NEW YORK STATE
TRIVIA

NEW YORK STATE TRIVIA

COMPILED BY MICHAEL J. MENDRICK

Rutledge Hill Press®
Nashville, Tennessee

Published by Rutledge Hill Press, a division of Thomas Nelson, Inc.,
P.O. Box 141000, Nashville, Tennessee 37214.

Typography by E. T. Lowe Publishing, Nashville, Tennessee.

Library of Congress Cataloging-in-Publication Data

Mendrick, Michael, 1958–
    New York State trivia / compiled by Michael Mendrick.
        p.   cm.
    ISBN 1-55853-534-9 (paperback)
    1. New York (State)—Miscellanea.   2. Questions and answers.
I. Title.
F119.M46   1997
974.7—dc21   97-34333
                                                                  CIP

Printed in the United States of America
    04 05 06 07 — 6 5 4 3

PREFACE

Once and for all, New York State is not just New York City! Although the peoples of New York State are generally proud of "the Big Apple," and are more than happy to consider it part of the Empire State, they can get a little sensitive when folks from the "other forty-nine" think this place is nothing but skyscrapers and cement. The following twelve hundred or so questions and answers about the *entire* state should help clear up some misperceptions and enlighten our neighbors around the world as to just how big, diverse, and fascinating New York State is!

To Becky, Daniel, and Jeremy. Thanks for being the only "answers" I'll ever need for the important questions in life.

TABLE OF CONTENTS

ACKNOWLEDGMENTS

A research project this extensive requires a lot of assistance from people and organizations that share a mutual interest in the subject along with sympathy for its author. I would like to thank the following for all their help in providing me with great information and healthy doses of support: David Brown, Penny Murphy, Concetta Youngblood, Buffalo Convention & Visitors Bureau, Ithaca/ Tompkins County Convention & Visitors Bureau, Empire State Development, New York City Convention & Visitors Bureau, Niagara Falls Convention & Visitors Bureau, Syracuse Convention & Visitors Bureau, Greater Rochester Visitors Association, Broome County Convention & Visitors Bureau, Westchester County Convention & Visitors Bureau, Lake Placid/Essex County Visitors Bureau, Albany County Convention & Visitors Bureau, Otsego County Chamber of Commerce, Schoharie County Chamber of Commerce, Cayuga County Office of Tourism, and the staff of the beautiful Saratoga Springs Public Library (for leaving the lights on for me).

GEOGRAPHY

Q. What is New York State's nickname?

A. The Empire State.

———⊗⊗⊗———

Q. What city in western New York has a ninety-five-foot waterfall near its downtown?

A. Rochester (High Falls).

———⊗⊗⊗———

Q. Which of the falls at Niagara are higher, the American Falls or the Canadian Falls?

A. The American Falls, at 190 feet, are five feet higher than the Canadian Falls.

———⊗⊗⊗———

Q. The Grand Canyon of the East is the nickname for what river gorge in western New York?

A. The Genesee River's six-hundred-foot-deep gorge in Letchworth State Park.

———⊗⊗⊗———

Q. New York State borders on what two Great Lakes?

A. Erie and Ontario.

Q. What two rivers separate New York State from Canada?

A. Niagara and Saint Lawrence.

Q. How long is the Niagara River?

A. Thirty-five miles, from Lake Erie into Lake Ontario.

Q. Where is the longest freshwater beach in the United States?

A. Plattsburgh, on Lake Champlain.

Q. With what foreign country does New York State share a border?

A. Canada.

Q. What Canadian city has the exact same name as a city located less than a mile away in New York State?

A. Niagara Falls.

Q. The second-busiest crossing point between the United States and Canada is spanned by what structure?

A. The Peace Bridge, in Buffalo.

Q. What is the highest elevation in New York State?

A. Mount Marcy (5,344 feet).

Q. How many miles of coastline does New York State have on the Atlantic Ocean?

A. 127.

———— ⊗∞o ————

Q. New York State covers how many square miles?

A. 49,108.

———— ⊗∞o ————

Q. Where does New York rank among the fifty states in total area?

A. Thirtieth.

———— ⊗∞o ————

Q. The geographic center of New York State is located where?

A. Near Madison, twelve miles south of Oneida and twenty-six miles southwest of Utica.

———— ⊗∞o ————

Q. The federal government owns what percentage of New York State land?

A. .69 percent.

———— ⊗∞o ————

Q. What is the population of New York State?

A. 18,136,081 (according to 1995 U.S. census estimates).

———— ⊗∞o ————

Q. In terms of population, where does New York rank among the fifty states?

A. Third (behind California and Texas).

Q. A 190-foot waterfall is near the downtown of what city in western New York State?

A. Niagara Falls (American Falls).

Q. What percentage of the population in New York State lives in metropolitan areas?

A. 91.8 percent.

Q. How many states border New York State?

A. Five (Vermont, Massachusetts, Connecticut, New Jersey, and Pennsylvania).

Q. What lake serves as a border between Vermont and New York State?

A. Champlain.

Q. At what age can a female New York resident legally marry with parental consent?

A. Fourteen.

Q. How long and wide is Lake Champlain?

A. 125 miles long by 14 miles wide.

Q. Where is New York State's one national seashore?

A. Fire Island, on Long Island.

Q. How wide are the American Falls at Niagara Falls?

A. 1,060 feet.

———— ∞∞∞ ————

Q. When was the Peace Bridge between Buffalo and Ontario, Canada, built?

A. 1927.

———— ∞∞∞ ————

Q. What is the capital of New York State?

A. Albany.

———— ∞∞∞ ————

Q. New York State's highest single waterfall is located where?

A. Taughannock Falls (not Niagara!), near Ithaca (215 feet).

———— ∞∞∞ ————

Q. How many miles of Lake Ontario shoreline border New York State?

A. Three hundred.

———— ∞∞∞ ————

Q. What is the source of the Hudson River?

A. Lake Tear-of-the-Clouds, in Essex County.

———— ∞∞∞ ————

Q. The Susquehanna River, which flows through southern New York State, is how long?

A. 444 miles.

Q. What is the source of the Susquehanna River?

A. Otsego Lake.

―∞―

Q. How many driving miles is it from Buffalo to New York City?

A. 393 miles.

―∞―

Q. What is the population of the Buffalo metropolitan area?

A. 1,189,237 (1994 Census Bureau estimate).

―∞―

Q. Shared by New York State and one other state, what national monument sits on an island?

A. The Statue of Liberty (shared with New Jersey).

―∞―

Q. Which U.S. president's Hyde Park home is now a national historic site?

A. Franklin D. Roosevelt's.

―∞―

Q. The Adirondack State Park occupies how many acres?

A. More than six million.

―∞―

Q. How many metropolitan areas in New York State have a population that exceeds one million people?

A. Three (New York City, Buffalo, and Rochester).

Q. What are the names of the five biggest Finger Lakes?

A. Canandaigua, Keuka, Seneca, Cayuga, and Skaneateles.

Q. Part of the border between New York and Pennsylvania is formed by what river?

A. Delaware.

Q. Bodies of water in what county comprise the source of the Delaware River?

A. Schoharie.

Q. How long and wide is Lake Erie?

A. 241 miles long by 57 miles wide.

Q. What is the highest mountain in the Catskill Mountains?

A. Slide Mountain (4,205 feet).

Q. New York State shares a border with which Canadian provinces?

A. Ontario and Quebec.

Q. Of the six million acres in the Adirondack Park, what percentage is privately owned?

A. 62 percent (3.7 million acres).

Q. The Catskill Mountains are part of what mountain chain?

A. The Appalachians.

———⚬⚬⚬———

Q. What is the westernmost lake in New York State?

A. Findley Lake (two miles from the Pennsylvania border).

———⚬⚬⚬———

Q. What state forms both part of the western and southern border of New York State?

A. Pennsylvania.

———⚬⚬⚬———

Q. New York State and Pennsylvania share what man-made lake?

A. The Allegheny Reservoir.

———⚬⚬⚬———

Q. What is the easternmost state park in New York?

A. Hither Hills State Park, near Montauk, Long Island.

———⚬⚬⚬———

Q. How long and wide is Lake Ontario?

A. 193 miles long by 53 miles wide.

———⚬⚬⚬———

Q. On a clear day, what city across Lake Ontario can be seen from Fort Niagara?

A. Toronto, Canada.

Q. Cornell University is located in what city?

A. Ithaca.

———⊗⊗⊗———

Q. Rochester's metropolitan area has how big a population?

A. 1,090,596 (1994 Census Bureau estimate).

———⊗⊗⊗———

Q. What river flows north through the city of Rochester on its way to Lake Ontario?

A. Genesee.

———⊗⊗⊗———

Q. For whom was Lake George named?

A. King George II of England.

———⊗⊗⊗———

Q. Lake Erie is how deep?

A. 210 feet, at its deepest.

———⊗⊗⊗———

Q. What interstate highways combine to form the New York State Thruway?

A. Interstate 87 and Interstate 90.

———⊗⊗⊗———

Q. How many communities named Rochester are there in the United States besides New York State's Rochester?

A. Eight.

Q. New York State consists of how many counties?

A. Sixty-two.

———∞∞∞———

Q. What was the estimated population in 1700 of the area that became New York State?

A. Twenty-six thousand.

———∞∞∞———

Q. How deep is Lake Ontario?

A. 802 feet, at its deepest point.

———∞∞∞———

Q. What is the county seat of Saratoga County?

A. Ballston Spa.

———∞∞∞———

Q. What is New York State's density of population?

A. 381 people per square mile (1990 census).

———∞∞∞———

Q. How many school districts are there in New York State?

A. 721.

———∞∞∞———

Q. New York State's public and private schools accommodated how many students, as of 1990?

A. More than three million (in elementary and secondary schools).

Q. Ithaca sits at the southern tip of what Finger Lake?

A. Cayuga.

Q. How many institutions of higher education exist in New York State?

A. 340 (1988).

Q. Which New York State county is largest in land area?

A. Saint Lawrence (2,728 square miles).

Q. Outside of New York City, what is the tallest building in the state?

A. The Corning Tower in Albany (589 feet; 44 floors).

Q. What is the longest suspension bridge in North America?

A. The Verrazano-Narrows Bridge, connecting Brooklyn to Staten Island (4,260-foot span).

Q. What is the fourth-biggest metropolitan region in New York State?

A. Albany-Schenectady-Troy (875,240, a 1994 Census Bureau estimate).

Q. The Hudson River is crossed by how many cantilever bridges?

A. Three (Tappan-Zee, Newburgh-Beacon, and Rip Van Winkle).

Q. What is the tallest building in Buffalo?

A. Marine Midland Center (529 feet; 40 stories).

———∞∞∞———

Q. What is the origin of the name for Ontario County?

A. It's a variation of the Iroquois word for "beautiful lake."

———∞∞∞———

Q. In what census year did New York State drop behind California as the nation's most-populous state?

A. 1970.

———∞∞∞———

Q. Where is the Rainbow Bridge?

A. It spans the Niagara River gorge at Niagara Falls.

———∞∞∞———

Q. What is the longest vehicle tunnel in New York State?

A. The Brooklyn-Battery tunnel, crossing beneath the East River in New York City (9,117 feet).

———∞∞∞———

Q. What upstate New York resort city is known as Queen of the Spas?

A. Saratoga Springs.

———∞∞∞———

Q. How many acres of forested land are there in New York State?

A. 18,775,000.

Q. In what year was Buffalo's original lighthouse built?

A. 1833.

Q. In what census year did New York State's population first go over the one-million mark?

A. 1820.

Q. What mountain, which you can drive to the top of, overlooks Lake George?

A. Prospect Mountain.

Q. What is the origin of the name for Niagara County?

A. It's a Native American word for "bisected bottomlands."

Q. How long was the original Erie Canal?

A. 363 miles, when completed in 1825.

Q. How many suspension bridges span the Hudson River?

A. Four (Verrazano-Narrows, George Washington, Bear Mountain, and Mid-Hudson).

Q. What is the county seat of Kings County?

A. Brooklyn.

Q. What is the lowest elevation in New York State?

A. Sea level, along the Atlantic Ocean shoreline.

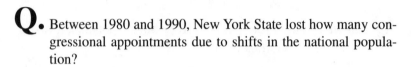

Q. Between 1980 and 1990, New York State lost how many congressional appointments due to shifts in the national population?

A. Three (from thirty-four to thirty-one seats).

Q. The 150-foot cliffs overlooking Lake Ontario near Sodus Bay go by what name?

A. Chimney Bluffs.

Q. For whom is the New York State Thruway named?

A. Thomas E. Dewey (a former governor of New York State).

Q. What is the tallest building in Rochester?

A. Xerox Tower (443 feet; 30 stories).

Q. Where does the Rip Van Winkle Bridge cross the Hudson River?

A. At Catskill.

Q. What percentage of New York State's total area consists of inland water?

A. 13.3 percent.

Q. What is the origin of the name for Schenectady?

A. It comes from the Mohawk word meaning "the other side of the pine lands."

Q. Is New York State considered a New England or Middle Atlantic state?

A. Middle Atlantic.

Q. What mountains lie along the eastern border of New York State?

A. The Taconic Range.

Q. How many years did it take to build the original Erie Canal?

A. Eight (1817 to 1825).

Q. What is the name of the cliffs that form the west bank of the Hudson River north of New York City?

A. The Palisades.

Q. The Adirondack Mountains are part of what mountain system?

A. The Canadian Shield.

Q. What is the name of the large lake northeast of Syracuse?

A. Oneida Lake.

Q. What is the origin of the name for Cattaraugus County?

A. It's a Seneca Indian word for "bad smelling banks."

Q. How many suspension bridges span the East River in New York City?

A. Four (Bronx-Whitestone, Williamsburg, Manhattan, and Triboro).

Q. Water flowing from the Allegheny River in New York State eventually empties into what body of water?

A. The Gulf of Mexico (via the Ohio and Mississippi Rivers).

Q. When was the New York State Barge Canal system completed?

A. 1918.

Q. The North Fork of Long Island is home to how many wineries?

A. More than a dozen.

Q. What is the southernmost lake within the Adirondack Park?

A. The Great Sacandaga.

Q. What county has more square miles of water within its boundaries than any other county in upstate New York?

A. Cayuga (in the Finger Lakes region).

Q. What arts and crafts-oriented community in the Hudson Valley shares the same name as a famous eastern U.S. ski resort?

A. The hamlet of Sugar Loaf.

───❈───

Q. What two lakes straddle parts of both Essex and Warren Counties?

A. George and Schroon.

───❈───

Q. What did Peck's Lake in Fulton County used to be?

A. Three ponds that were flooded to form the lake.

───❈───

Q. What is the lowest point below sea level in the contiguous forty-eight states?

A. The bottom of Lake Champlain (314 feet below sea level, off Split Rock).

───❈───

Q. What county is the state's largest in population?

A. Kings (2,244,031, according to a 1994 census estimate).

───❈───

Q. What is the world's longest toll superhighway?

A. The New York State Thruway (558 miles).

───❈───

Q. How many airports are there in New York State?

A. Nearly five hundred (commercial and general aviation).

Q. What is the origin of the name for Genesee County?

A. It's a Seneca Indian word meaning "good valley."

———∞∞∞———

Q. How long is Lake George?

A. Thirty-two miles.

———∞∞∞———

Q. How many state colleges are there in the State University of New York system?

A. Thirteen.

———∞∞∞———

Q. Where are the four university centers of the State University of New York?

A. Albany, Binghamton, Buffalo, and Stony Brook.

———∞∞∞———

Q. The New York Maritime College is located in what city?

A. Syracuse.

———∞∞∞———

Q. What is the total length of the New York State Barge Canal system?

A. 525 miles (including the original Erie Canal).

———∞∞∞———

Q. What is the largest university in the SUNY system?

A. SUNY at Buffalo (24,500 students).

Q. Downtown Syracuse is bordered by what body of water?

A. Onondaga Lake.

———∞———

Q. Clinton's Ditch was the original nickname given what engineering marvel that opened in 1825?

A. The Erie Canal.

———∞———

Q. The suspension bridge at Ogdensburg linking New York State and Canada is how long?

A. 1,120 feet (across the Saint Lawrence River).

———∞———

Q. How many of the Adirondack mountains exceed four thousand feet in elevation?

A. Forty-two.

———∞———

Q. Where was the first drive-through bank window in America?

A. At the Merchant's National Bank in Syracuse (in 1941).

———∞———

Q. How long is the span of the Tappan-Zee Bridge that crosses the Hudson River near Tarrytown?

A. 1,212 feet.

———∞———

Q. Where was the country's first wooden plank road?

A. The Hemlock Highway, from Central Square in Syracuse to Salina.

Q. What interstate highway runs from the Canadian border through Syracuse and Binghamton and into Pennsylvania?

A. Interstate 81.

———❈———

Q. The nation's only upside-down traffic light can be found in what New York State locale?

A. At the intersection of Tompkins Street and Lowell Avenue in Syracuse.

———❈———

Q. How many farms are there in New York State?

A. 32,306 (as of 1992).

———❈———

Q. How many locks were there in the original Erie Canal?

A. Eighty-three.

———❈———

Q. What is New York State's leading agricultural product?

A. Dairy products (with sales of $1.43 billion in 1992).

———❈———

Q. From what city does Syracuse take its name?

A. Siracusa, on the island of Sicily in Italy.

———❈———

Q. What is New York State's motto?

A. Excelsior ("Ever upward").

Q. Water flowing from the Genesee River in New York State eventually empties into what body of water?

A. The Gulf of Saint Lawrence (through Lake Ontario and the Saint Lawrence Seaway).

Q. What is the average size of a farm in New York State?

A. 231 acres.

Q. What waterway connects Lake Ontario with the Barge Canal?

A. The Oswego Canal.

Q. How many bushels of corn are harvested annually in New York State?

A. 47,702,382 (in 1992).

Q. As a boy, twenty-fourth U.S. president Grover Cleveland was known to enjoy what swimming hole near Syracuse?

A. Limestone Creek.

Q. What is Interstate 87 north of Albany called?

A. The Adirondack Northway.

Q. What percentage of New York State's population is under the age of eighteen?

A. 25 percent (1995 census estimate).

Q. How many lakes and ponds are there in the Adirondack Park?

A. Approximately twenty-eight hundred.

———

Q. What toll road was constructed in 1936 as a memorial to World War I servicemen?

A. Whiteface Memorial Highway (to the top of 4,866-foot Whiteface Mountain).

———

Q. How long is the Hudson River?

A. 306 miles.

———

Q. For whom is the airport in Syracuse named?

A. John Hancock.

———

Q. How far does the Raquette River travel before flowing into the Saint Lawrence River?

A. Approximately two hundred miles.

———

Q. When it is 8:00 A.M. in New York City at the southeastern corner of the state, what time is it in Niagara Falls at the western end of the state?

A. 8:00 A.M. (both are in the Eastern Time Zone).

———

Q. How many head of cattle are there in New York State?

A. 1,470,610 (as of 1992).

Q. What interstate highway links Schenectady to Binghamton?

A. Interstate 88.

Q. For whom was Franklin County named in 1808?

A. Benjamin Franklin.

Q. How many islands are there in Lake George?

A. 225.

Q. What New York State park is as big as Yellowstone, Grand Canyon, Yosemite, Everglades, and Great Smoky Mountains National Parks combined?

A. The Adirondack Park.

Q. A 7,400-foot cable railway ran from what village to the top of Prospect Mountain from 1895 to 1903?

A. Lake George.

Q. What county has the smallest population in New York State?

A. Hamilton County (5,208 according to a 1995 census estimate).

Q. What is the largest U.S. lake east of the Rockies that sits at an elevation of at least 1,750 feet?

A. Lake Placid.

Q. What mountains contain the oldest rocks in North America?

A. The Adirondacks.

Q. What is Rochester's promotional nickname?

A. The World's Image Centre.

Q. How many Electoral College votes does New York State represent?

A. Thirty-three (based on the 1990 census).

Q. How many miles of rivers and streams are there in the Adirondack Park?

A. More than thirty thousand.

Q. What are known as the Twin Towers in New York City?

A. The 110-story towers of the World Trade Center.

Q. At what age can a male New York resident legally marry with parental consent?

A. Sixteen.

Q. What city in New York State is known as the Big Apple?

A. New York City.

Q. How many of the five biggest banks in the United States are based in New York City?

A. Four.

———∞———

Q. New York City ranks where among the nation's busiest ports?

A. Third, after South Louisiana (includes New Orleans) and Houston.

———∞———

Q. How many registered vehicles per one thousand residents are there in New York State?

A. 561.

———∞———

Q. What Syracuse-based company is the nation's largest producer of fine quality commercial china?

A. Syracuse China.

———∞———

Q. What city used to be known as the Flour City, then the Flower City?

A. Rochester.

———∞———

Q. Where is Canisius College located?

A. Buffalo.

———∞———

Q. What airport was ranked eighth-busiest in the United States in 1995?

A. JFK International, in New York City (30,237,723 passengers).

Q. What body of water does the village of Lake Placid overlook?

A. Mirror Lake.

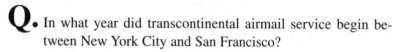

Q. In what year did transcontinental airmail service begin between New York City and San Francisco?

A. 1921.

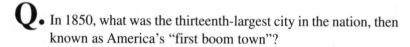

Q. In 1850, what was the thirteenth-largest city in the nation, then known as America's "first boom town"?

A. Rochester (36,403 population).

Q. For what is Manhattan named?

A. The Man-a-hat-a Indians (who sold it to the Dutch for twenty-four dollars' worth of goods).

Q. Who were the first inhabitants of New York State?

A. The Algonquins (beginning about A.D. 1000).

Q. What Westchester County road is considered the world's first public automobile parkway?

A. The Bronx River Parkway.

Q. How many public libraries are there in New York State?

A. 758.

Q. How many cities are situated within the 9,375-square-mile Adirondack Park?

A. None (only towns and villages).

———∞———

Q. At what age can a New York resident legally drink?

A. Twenty-one.

———∞———

Q. How many hogs and pigs are there in New York State?

A. 90,282 (as of 1992).

———∞———

Q. What was the first planned suburban development in the United States?

A. Mount Vernon.

———∞———

Q. Host site of the 1954 National Governor's Conference, what resort hotel is listed in the National Register of Historic Places?

A. The Sagamore on Lake George.

———∞———

Q. Lake George was originally given what French name?

A. *Lac du Saint Sacrament* (Lake of the Blessed Sacrament).

———∞———

Q. By what nickname is Westchester County known?

A. The Golden Apple.

Q. What county is the birthplace of Endicott-Johnson shoes?

A. Broome County.

Q. The village of Saranac Lake overlooks what body of water?

A. Lake Flower.

Q. How many people are employed by Eastman Kodak in Rochester?

A. Approximately thirty-four thousand.

Q. In what town was Martin Van Buren, former New York governor and U.S. president, born?

A. Kinderhook (outside of Albany).

Q. What is considered "the first American college," since it was the first to be chartered after the American Revolution?

A. Union College, in Schenectady.

Q. The American and Canadian falls at Niagara are separated by what piece of land?

A. Goat Island.

Q. The island of Manhattan occupies how many square miles?

A. 22.7.

Q. How many flights took off and landed at the three New York City area airports in 1995?

A. 1.1 million.

———— ❦ ————

Q. What is the fifth-largest metropolitan area in New York State?

A. Syracuse (753,980, according to a 1994 census estimate).

———— ❦ ————

Q. How many licensed taxis are there in New York City?

A. Nearly twelve thousand.

———— ❦ ————

Q. What two roadways originate in Albany and were among the first toll roads in New York State, dating back to the early 1800s?

A. Albany-Schenectady Road (now N.Y. 5) and Great Western Turnpike (now U.S. 20).

———— ❦ ————

Q. How many passengers ride the Staten Island Ferry on an average day?

A. Fifty-nine thousand.

———— ❦ ————

Q. How many skyscrapers are there in New York City?

A. Approximately two hundred.

———— ❦ ————

Q. What river appears on the state seal?

A. The Hudson River.

Q. How many square miles does Long Island consist of?

A. 1,723.

Q. Where is the oldest church pulpit in America?

A. In the First Church of Albany (it dates back to 1656).

Q. What geological wonder is located at the base of Niagara's Bridal Veil Falls?

A. The Cave of the Winds.

Q. How many tourism regions are identified in the "I Love New York" program?

A. Eleven.

Q. For whom is the city of Yonkers named?

A. Jonkheer Van de Donck (Dutch landowner).

Q. What is the minimum age for a person to be elected governor of New York?

A. Thirty.

Q. Where was the first Shaker settlement in America?

A. In Albany County (in 1776).

Q. How many identical four-room houses were built in Levittown, the nation's first subdivision, between 1947 and 1951?

A. 17,447.

Q. How many miles of railway are operated in New York?

A. 2,427 (in 1991).

Q. How many federal Indian reservations are there in New York?

A. Six.

Q. Where is the only place in the world you can buy a Spiedie sandwich?

A. Broome County.

Q. How many private colleges and universities are there in New York?

A. 236.

Q. Albany's Union Train Station opened in what year?

A. 1900 (serving until 1968).

Q. What Adirondack town is known as the Home of the High Peaks?

A. Keene.

Q. How many people per square mile live in Hamilton County, the least-populous county in the state?

A. Approximately three.

———⊗⊗⊗———

Q. During the summer tourist season, by how many times does the population of Hamilton County in the Adirondacks multiply?

A. Twelve (from five thousand to more than sixty thousand).

———⊗⊗⊗———

Q. What is the most sparsely populated town in New York?

A. Morehouse (106 people in 191 square miles).

———⊗⊗⊗———

Q. The Federal Highway Administration named what New York highway "America's Most Scenic" for 1966?

A. Interstate 87 (Adirondack Northway) north of Lake George.

———⊗⊗⊗———

Q. What was the first municipal airport in America?

A. Lindbergh Field, in Albany (1928).

———⊗⊗⊗———

Q. What American location stands next to the Canadian Falls at Niagara?

A. Terrapin Point, on Goat Island.

———⊗⊗⊗———

Q. Where is former U.S. president Chester Arthur buried?

A. Albany Rural Cemetery.

Q. The only tunnel in the state that runs under the Erie Canal can be found where?

A. Medina.

Q. What castle in the Saint Lawrence River stands unfinished after two million dollars of construction, halted in 1904 as the result of the tragic death of the owner's wife?

A. Boldt Castle, on Heart Island.

Q. What place is nicknamed Queen City of the Hudson?

A. Yonkers.

Q. Of how many islands do the Thousand Islands actually consist?

A. Approximately eighteen hundred.

Q. Where is the shortest international vehicular bridge in the world, measuring only forty-two feet long and five feet wide?

A. At Zavicon Island in the Saint Lawrence River (connecting the United States and Canada).

Q. Which Finger Lake is shaped like a *Y*?

A. Keuka Lake.

Q. The Prudential Building, one of the world's first skyscrapers, was built in what city?

A. Buffalo (in 1896).

Q. What are the predominant peoples around the community of Conewango Valley in western New York?

A. The Amish.

———⊗⊗⊙———

Q. Who coined the word *Adirondacks* for the mountainous region of northern New York?

A. Professor Ebenezer Emmons (during a geological survey in 1837).

———⊗⊗⊙———

Q. For whom was Broome County named in 1806?

A. John Broome, who was lieutenant governor at the time.

———⊗⊗⊙———

Q. How many miles of roads, streets, and highways are there in New York?

A. 111,242 (in 1990).

———⊗⊗⊙———

Q. In what year was Buffalo's thirty-story art deco city hall building completed?

A. 1929.

———⊗⊗⊙———

Q. What is the origin of the name for Chautauqua County?

A. It's a Seneca Indian word meaning "where the fish was taken out."

———⊗⊗⊙———

Q. For whom was Clinton County named in 1788?

A. George Clinton (the first governor of the state).

Q. When was the Adirondack Park created by law?

A. 1892.

───⊗∞───

Q. What Finger Lakes community at the north shore of Seneca Lake is home to Hobart and William Smith colleges?

A. Geneva.

───⊗∞───

Q. For whom was Cortland County named in 1808?

A. Pierre Van Cortlandt (the state's first lieutenant governor).

───⊗∞───

Q. What naval ships are moored at the Buffalo Naval & Military Park?

A. Destroyer USS *The Sullivans*, Missile Cruiser USS *Little Rock*, Submarine USS *Croaker*.

───⊗∞───

Q. For whom was Warren County named in 1813?

A. General John Warren (who was killed in the Battle of Bunker Hill).

───⊗∞───

Q. What scenic route covers 454 miles along the shoreline of Lake Erie, the Niagara River, Lake Ontario, and the Saint Lawrence River?

A. The Seaway Trail.

───⊗∞───

Q. During the American Revolution, Native American women and children used what island in Canandaigua Lake as a hiding place?

A. Squaw Island.

Q. What is the name given the huge log homes built in the early 1900s in northern New York for America's wealthy families such as the Whitneys, Vanderbilts, and Rockefellers?

A. Adirondack Great Camps.

Q. What Finger Lakes community has two significant colleges situated on hills overlooking the city (and each other)?

A. Ithaca (Cornell University and Ithaca College).

Q. For whom was Dutchess [sic] County named in 1683?

A. The Duchess of York (wife of James II).

Q. What is the nickname of Buffalo?

A. The Queen City.

Q. In what city is Vassar College located?

A. Poughkeepsie.

Q. The Broad Street Bridge in Rochester used to be what other structure?

A. The Erie Canal Aqueduct.

ENTERTAINMENT

C H A P T E R   T W O

Q. Buffalo was the location for filming of what 1980 movie starring James Caan and Danny Aiello?

A. *Hide in Plain Sight.*

———

Q. What brother and sister have starred in recent TV sitcoms and were born in Rye?

A. Jason and Justine Bateman.

———

Q. What 1980 film starring Fred Astaire, Douglas Fairbanks Jr., and John Houseman was filmed in Saratoga Springs?

A. *Ghost Story.*

———

Q. Saratoga Springs is the primary residence for what famous socialite and former actress?

A. Mary Lou Whitney (widow of Cornelius Vanderbilt Whitney).

———

Q. What 1997 action film was so highly anticipated that a cinema in New York City played it on six different screens with showings every thirty minutes?

A. *The Lost World: Jurassic Park.*

Q. What stage and film star known for his one-man show as Harry S. Truman was born in White Plains?

A. James Whitmore.

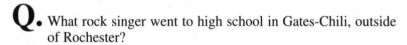

Q. What rock singer went to high school in Gates-Chili, outside of Rochester?

A. Lou Grammatico (Lou Gramm, lead singer for the group Foreigner).

Q. Massapequa on Long Island is home to what four brother actors?

A. The Baldwins (Alec, Stephen, Daniel, and William).

Q. The comedy classic *Tootsie* starring Dustin Hoffman was partially filmed in what region of New York?

A. The Hudson Valley.

Q. What star of the film *Love Story* was born in Pound Ridge?

A. Ali MacGraw.

Q. What famous showman and promoter visited Paul Smith's hotel near Lower Saint Regis Lake and had a pond named after him?

A. P. T. Barnum.

Q. How many movie theater screens are there in the Albany-Schenectady-Troy metropolitan area?

A. Forty-five.

Q. Where is Santa's Workshop theme park located?

A. North Pole, New York (actually Wilmington).

Q. What *Cybill* TV sitcom sidekick was born in Buffalo?

A. Christine Baranski.

Q. What Wild West-themed amusement park is located in North Hudson?

A. Frontier Town.

Q. What is the only zoo in the Adirondack region?

A. Adirondack Animal Land, near Mayfield.

Q. How many people annually attend the Corn Hill Arts Festival in Rochester?

A. Approximately two hundred fifty thousand.

Q. What bad boy of films such as *9½ Weeks* was born in Schenectady?

A. Mickey Rourke.

Q. At what attraction can you see World War I vintage warplanes do battle in mock dogfights?

A. The Rhinebeck Aerodrome, outside Rhinebeck.

Q. The mythical town of Bedford Falls in the classic film *It's a Wonderful Life* was supposedly based on what upstate community?

A. Seneca Falls.

Q. In what northern New York community did Kate Smith, famous as the singer of "God Bless America," keep a summer home?

A. Lake Placid.

Q. What is the name of New York State's only casino?

A. Turning Stone, located near Verona.

Q. Where was Kirk Douglas born?

A. Amsterdam, New York.

Q. The 1996 thriller *The Juror*, starring Alec Baldwin and Demi Moore, was shot in what Hudson River community?

A. Nyack.

Q. What is the only amusement park in the state to border Lake Ontario?

A. Seabreeze Amusement Park, in Irondequoit.

Q. What is upstate New York's largest professional theater?

A. The Merry-Go-Round Playhouse, in Auburn.

Q. The TV show *The Commish* was modeled after the former police chief of what Westchester town?

A. Rye.

―∞―

Q. What Westchester amusement park was the site of some filming for the movies *Big* and *Radio Days*?

A. Playland Amusement Park.

―∞―

Q. Who is the composer and folksinger who onced lived in Scarborough and whose 1944 album contained the first recorded versions of "Greensleeves" and "The Twelve Days of Christmas"?

A. Tom Glazer.

―∞―

Q. What notorious punk rocker was evicted from the Brownies during her youth in Rochester in the 1950s?

A. Wendy O. Williams.

―∞―

Q. Cafe Lena in Saratoga Springs was where what popular 1972 song made its debut?

A. "American Pie," by Don McLean.

―∞―

Q. What famous TV sidekick attended high school in Rochester in the 1930s?

A. Jay Silverheels (who played Tonto on *The Lone Ranger*).

―∞―

Q. Rob Morrow, star of television's quirky *Northern Exposure*, was born in what New York State community?

A. New Rochelle.

Q. What New York City cop was the inspiration for the movie *The French Connection*?

A. Eddie Egan.

Q. Who was the last Miss New York State to win the Miss America pageant?

A. Vanessa Williams (in 1984).

Q. What lovable TV lush who starred on *Dean Martin Celebrity Roasts* lived in Rush outside of Rochester for many years?

A. Foster Brooks.

Q. *Scent of a Woman*, the 1992 film that earned Al Pacino the Best Actor Academy Award, filmed the key boarding school scenes where?

A. At the Emma Willard School, in Troy.

Q. What town was the birthplace of Tim Daly, star of the long-running TV sitcom *Wings*?

A. Suffern.

Q. Schenectady-born Ann B. Davis portrayed what popular TV sitcom character that featured a blended family of three boys and three girls?

A. Alice, the housekeeper on television's *The Brady Bunch*.

Q. Off-the-wall comedian Bobcat Goldthwait was born in what upstate New York community?

A. Syracuse.

Q. The principal scenes for what 1997 movie starring and directed by Robert Redford were shot in Saratoga County?

A. *The Horse Whisperer.*

———∞∞∞———

Q. What half of a famous comedy team managed a theater in Rochester during the 1920s?

A. Bud Abbott (of Abbott & Costello).

———∞∞∞———

Q. The Mohonk Mountain House resort was the location for the filming of what 1994 movie starring Anthony Hopkins and Matthew Broderick?

A. *The Road to Wellville.*

———∞∞∞———

Q. The TV shows *Rescue 911*, *America's Most Wanted*, and *Unsolved Mysteries* have all filmed in what region of New York?

A. The Finger Lakes.

———∞∞∞———

Q. What famous jazz musician was born in Rochester in 1907?

A. Cab Calloway.

———∞∞∞———

Q. What was the original name given New Yorker Kirk Douglas?

A. Issur Danielovitch.

———∞∞∞———

Q. Where and when was *Phonofilm*, the first sound-on-film motion picture, shown?

A. At the Rivoli Theater in New York City (in April 1923).

Q. Who was the late Random House president and panelist on TV's *What's My Line* who made his home in Mount Kisco?

A. Bennett Cerf.

Q. The pennant of what New York State college was displayed in the malt shop on the TV series *Happy Days*?

A. Iona.

Q. What took place on farmland near Bethel August 15–17, 1969?

A. The Woodstock music festival.

Q. While her husband attended medical school, what movie actress spent 1941 in Rochester?

A. Ingrid Bergman.

Q. Where did TV and movie actor Alan Alda attend high school?

A. Archbishop Stepinac High School, in Westchester County.

Q. What is the birthplace of film actor Denzel Washington?

A. Mount Vernon.

Q. Union College in Schenectady was the location for filming of key scenes in what 1973 movie starring Robert Redford and Barbara Streisand?

A. *The Way We Were.*

Q. Caroga Lake is bordered by what amusement park?

A. Sherman's Park.

———∞∞∞———

Q. What 1988 thriller starring Lukas Haas of *Witness* fame was filmed in Rochester?

A. *Lady in White.*

———∞∞∞———

Q. Jane Alexander, Yoko Ono, Carly Simon, and Barbara Walters all attended what New York State college?

A. Sarah Lawrence, in Westchester.

———∞∞∞———

Q. What New York State event is one of the oldest continuously running rodeos in the United States?

A. The Painted Pony Rodeo, in Lake Luzerne.

———∞∞∞———

Q. What TV maestro who urged viewers to "sing along" was born in Rochester in 1911?

A. Mitch Miller.

———∞∞∞———

Q. What downstate community was the site of some filming for the Michael J. Fox movie *The Secret of My Success*?

A. Somers.

———∞∞∞———

Q. What Westchester resident was the composer of *Little Shop of Horrors*, *The Little Mermaid*, and *Beauty and the Beast*?

A. Alan Menken.

Q. Tony Award–winning actress Mercedes Ruehl is a graduate of what New York State college?

A. The College of New Rochelle.

Q. Hastings-on-Hudson was the home of what two stars of *The Wizard of Oz*?

A. Billie Burke and Frank Morgan.

Q. What film starring Daniel Day-Lewis was based on historical events that took place around Lake George?

A. *Last of the Mohicans.*

Q. What professional opera company based in the Adirondack region celebrated its thirty-fifth anniversary in 1997?

A. The Lake George Opera Festival.

Q. What was Rochester-born 1950s TV star Hugh O'Brian's given name?

A. Hugh Krampke.

Q. The 1977 sports comedy *Slap Shot*, starring Paul Newman, was filmed in what two upstate cities?

A. Syracuse and Utica.

Q. What actor, who played the captain on *The Love Boat,* was born in Mount Kisco?

A. Gavin MacLeod.

Q. How many rides and attractions are there at the Great Escape theme park in Lake George?

A. 125.

———— ∞ ————

Q. Where was the 1988 film *Masquerade*, starring Rob Lowe and Meg Tilly, shot?

A. Long Island.

———— ∞ ————

Q. Actor and director Carl Reiner lived in what community from 1953 to 1960?

A. New Rochelle (the fictional home of Rob Petrie from Reiner's *The Dick Van Dyke Show*).

———— ∞ ————

Q. In 1989, Meryl Streep and Roseanne Barr filmed what comedy movie on Long Island?

A. *She-Devil.*

———— ∞ ————

Q. Where did furry TV star Rin Tin Tin live and bark?

A. Mount Vernon.

———— ∞ ————

Q. Jonathan Winters and his many comic personas once lived in what community?

A. Hastings-on-Hudson.

———— ∞ ————

Q. What film actress and star of movies such as *The Big Chill* and *Fatal Attraction* has made her home in Westchester County?

A. Glenn Close.

Q. The long-running TV sitcom *The Facts of Life* was set in what city?

A. Peekskill.

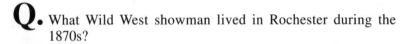

Q. What Wild West showman lived in Rochester during the 1870s?

A. Buffalo Bill Cody.

Q. The mayor of what city presided over the marriage of Marilyn Monroe and playwright Arthur Miller?

A. White Plains.

Q. What Long Island native was the star of the movie *The Karate Kid*?

A. Ralph Macchio.

Q. What New Rochelle address did the Petrie Family of *The Dick Van Dyke Show* have?

A. 448 Bonnie Meadow Road.

Q. Kimberly Williams, the actress who starred in the 1991 film *Father of the Bride* with Steve Martin, attended what high school?

A. Rye High School.

Q. What was New York City–born-and-raised film star and director Woody Allen's given name?

A. Allen Konigsberg.

Q. What was the name of the amusement park that once bordered the shores of Canandaigua Lake?

A. Roseland Park.

Q. Who wrote the play *Lost in Yonkers*?

A. Neil Simon.

Q. Mount Vernon was the home of what famous actor and director, whose credits include *Guess Who's Coming to Dinner*?

A. Sidney Poitier.

Q. What jazz great and composer of "Feels So Good" was born in Rochester?

A. Chuck Mangione.

Q. Where were parts of the film *Ragtime* shot?

A. Mount Kisco.

Q. What food festival is recognized as the second-largest "Taste of" event in the nation?

A. Taste of Buffalo (with fifty-five participating restaurants).

Q. As of 1997, where was the only Hard Rock Cafe in upstate New York located?

A. Niagara Falls.

Q. Ed Sullivan began his career by writing for the local newspaper in what community?

A. Port Chester.

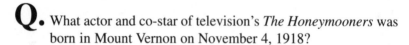

Q. What actor and co-star of television's *The Honeymooners* was born in Mount Vernon on November 4, 1918?

A. Art Carney.

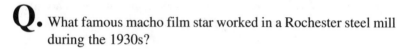

Q. What famous macho film star worked in a Rochester steel mill during the 1930s?

A. Kirk Douglas.

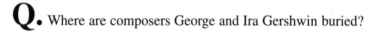

Q. Where are composers George and Ira Gershwin buried?

A. Westchester Hills Cemetery.

Q. Where is New York's Fantasy Island?

A. On Grand Island (it's an amusement park).

Q. Where is singer and actress Judy Garland of *Wizard of Oz* fame buried?

A. Ferncliff Mausoleum, in Westchester County.

Q. What writer and director known for television's *The Twilight Zone* grew up in Broome County?

A. Rod Serling.

Q. Pop singing star Mariah Carey was born in what Long Island community?

A. Huntington.

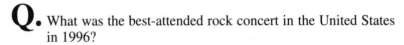

Q. What was the best-attended rock concert in the United States in 1996?

A. The Clifford Ball, outside of Plattsburgh, featuring Phish (120,000 spectators).

Q. What upstate New York community was the location for more than one hundred silent films during the 1910s?

A. Ithaca (produced by Wharton Studios).

Q. Where is showman Florenz Ziegfield (of *The Ziegfield Follies*) buried?

A. Kensico Cemetery, in Westchester County.

Q. What star of the television prime time soap *Knots Landing* was born in Albany?

A. William Devane.

Q. At what Saratoga club did singer Joan Osbourne play before she hit it big in the music business?

A. The Metro.

Q. What actress (the first Mrs. Tom Cruise) started her career with the Rochester Community Players?

A. Mimi (Kennedy) Rogers.

Q. How many times has a Miss New York State won the Miss America pageant?

A. Three (Bess Myerson in 1945, Tawney Godin in 1976, and Vanessa Williams in 1984).

Q. What long-time character actor and victim of misunderstanding in the film *Tootsie* was born in Highland Falls?

A. Charles Durning.

Q. Jesse White, the actor best known as the lonely Maytag repairman, was born where?

A. Buffalo.

Q. What former child actor, who grew up to be an entertainment legend, lived in Rochester during the 1920s?

A. Mickey Rooney.

Q. What was one of the largest theaters in the world when it opened in 1931?

A. The Palace Theater, in Albany.

Q. Where was original Mousketeer and beach movie film star Annette Funnicello born?

A. Utica.

Q. Before he became a circus promoter, where did P. T. Barnum house his Freak Show?

A. At what is now the Key Bank Building in Albany.

Q. Where and when was New York's first state fair?

A. In Otsego County in 1816.

———∞∞∞———

Q. How many people attend the New York State Fair each year in Syracuse?

A. More than eight hundred thousand.

———∞∞∞———

Q. New Rochelle native Bob Denver starred in what 1960s TV hit?

A. *Gilligan's Island.*

———∞∞∞———

Q. What ageless rock-and-roll promoter and television personality was born in Mount Vernon on November 30, 1929?

A. Dick Clark.

———∞∞∞———

Q. What huge multinational exposition was held in Queens in 1939?

A. The World's Fair.

———∞∞∞———

Q. The Robert Redford movie *The Natural* was filmed in what upstate New York stadium?

A. War Memorial Stadium, in Buffalo.

———∞∞∞———

Q. What is the seating capacity of the Darien Lake amphitheater, home of summer outdoor concerts by national performers?

A. Twenty thousand.

Q. Who first used the term *the Big Apple* for New York City?

A. Jazz musicians during the 1930s.

———— ∞∞ ————

Q. What star of the TV sitcom *Third Rock from the Sun* was born in Rochester on October 19, 1945?

A. John Lithgow.

———— ∞∞ ————

Q. Where is bandleader Tommy Dorsey buried?

A. Kensico Cemetery, in Westchester County.

———— ∞∞ ————

Q. How many Broadway theaters are there in New York City?

A. Thirty-five.

———— ∞∞ ————

Q. What reclusive star of silent films died in Rochester in 1985?

A. Louise Brooks.

———— ∞∞ ————

Q. How many movies were filmed in New York City in 1995?

A. 175.

———— ∞∞ ————

Q. On July 7, 1962, what future movie star of such films as *Rainman* and *A Few Good Men* was born in Syracuse?

A. Tom Cruise.

Q. When did the Saratoga Performing Arts Center amphitheater open?

A. 1966.

———∞———

Q. What was the first school in the nation to train men to play the part of Santa Claus?

A. The Santa Claus School, in Albion (1937).

———∞———

Q. The town in the film *Nobody's Fool*, starring Paul Newman, was supposedly modeled after what upstate town?

A. Ballston Spa.

———∞———

Q. What daytime TV actress and record-setting Emmy nominee (for most losses) was born in Scarsdale on December 23, 1950?

A. Susan Lucci.

———∞———

Q. What upstate theme park has a major outdoor concert amphitheater?

A. Darien Lake.

———∞———

Q. What 1993 Martin Scorcese film starring Daniel Day-Lewis was filmed in Troy?

A. *The Age of Innocence.*

———∞———

Q. *Saratoga Trunk* was the last film of what female movie star, who died during the making of the movie in 1941?

A. Jean Harlow.

Q. The 1982 comedy *Best Friends* was filmed in Buffalo and starred what actor and actress?

A. Burt Reynolds and Goldie Hawn.

———

Q. The Genesee River gorge was the setting for the filming of what legendary soap opera episode?

A. The return of Luke and Laura to *General Hospital*.

———

Q. The 1994 film *Canadian Bacon*, one of the last starring comedian John Candy before his death, was shot in what city?

A. Niagara Falls.

———

Q. Who was the first person to ever cross Niagara Falls on a tightrope (June 30, 1859)?

A. Frenchman Jean Francois Gravelet (aka Emile Blondin).

———

Q. Comedienne and TV talk show Emmy-winner Rosie O'Donnell was born where?

A. Commack.

———

Q. What natural attraction in western New York did David Copperfield once make "disappear" during one of his television specials?

A. Niagara Falls.

———

Q. The 1995 movie remake of *Sabrina*, starring Harrison Ford and Julia Ormond, was filmed in what area of Long Island?

A. Glen Cove.

Q. What popular, then infamous, children's TV show performer was born in Peekskill on August 27, 1952?

A. Pee-Wee Herman (Paul Reubens).

———

Q. Edward Burns wrote, directed, starred in, and filmed what 1995 comedy movie on Long Island?

A. *The Brothers McMullen.*

———

Q. Emmy-winner David Hyde Pierce, who plays Niles on the TV sitcom *Frasier*, grew up in what city?

A. Saratoga Springs.

———

Q. In what year was the first Saranac Lake Winter Carnival held?

A. 1897.

———

Q. What former TV sidekick of Mary Tyler Moore and later star of her own show, *Rhoda*, was born in Suffern?

A. Valerie Harper.

———

Q. Troy was the location for filming what 1988 drama starring Jack Nicholson and Meryl Streep?

A. *Ironweed.*

———

Q. Where did actress Cybill Shepherd attend college?

A. The College of New Rochelle.

Q. Which of the original "video jocks" on MTV was born in Albany?

A. Martha Quinn.

———⌘———

Q. Bob Keeshan, television's Captain Kangaroo, was born in what town?

A. Lynbrook.

———⌘———

Q. *Wolf*, the 1994 thriller starring Jack Nicholson and Michelle Pfeiffer, was filmed in what region of New York?

A. Long Island.

———⌘———

Q. In 1996, what did the fifteen-thousand-seat Knickerbocker Arena in Albany change its name to?

A. The Pepsi Arena.

———⌘———

Q. In what year did New York City host its second World's Fair?

A. 1964.

———⌘———

Q. What is the distinguishing feature of the Starlite Music Theatre in Latham?

A. The twenty-eight hundred seats form a complete circle around the rotating stage.

———⌘———

Q. Buffalo is the birthplace of what well-known piano-playing political satirist?

A. Mark Russell.

Q. What is the name of the sightseeing cruise boat that plies the waters of Raquette Lake?

A. The *W. W. Durant*.

Q. What is the name of the laser, light, and sound show in the Genesee River gorge at High Falls in Rochester?

A. *River of Light*.

Q. At what Niagara area entertainment complex will you see summer theater "in the round," featuring touring musical and comedy artists?

A. Melody Fair Theater.

Q. Film director Peter Bogdanovich (*The Last Picture Show*) was born in what town?

A. Kingston.

Q. In what community did Jay Leno deliver his first monologue during elementary school?

A. New Rochelle.

Q. What is the name of the sightseeing paddleboat that cruises the waters of Chautauqua Lake?

A. The *Chautauqua Belle*.

Q. How many concertgoers can be seated inside at Artpark in Lewiston?

A. Twenty-three hundred (and room for several thousand more on the lawn).

Q. What 1990 film starring Jeremy Irons and based on a famous murder case was filmed on Long Island?

A. *Reversal of Fortune.*

Q. Fashion model Beverly Johnson was born in what western New York city?

A. Buffalo.

Q. *Fear No Evil*, a 1981 horror movie, was filmed in what city?

A. Rochester.

Q. Marlin Perkins, host of TV's *Wild Kingdom*, was once curator for what upstate zoo?

A. The Buffalo Zoological Gardens.

Q. What event is recognized by the American Bus Association as one of the top one hundred in the United States for tour groups?

A. The Festival of Lights, in Niagara Falls.

Q. What Erie Canal cruiseboat is named after a famous daredevil, who lost his life jumping over the Upper Genesee Falls on a horse in 1829?

A. The *Sam Patch.*

Q. At what Lake Ontario community will you find jousting matches and court jesters?

A. In Sterling, during the Sterling Renaissance Festival.

Q. What island was given away by Bill Cullen in 1964 on the TV game show *The Price is Right*?

A. The Price is Right Island, in the Saint Lawrence River.

———⊗⊗⊙———

Q. What type of show takes place in the river gorge at Watkins Glen?

A. The laser light show *Timespell*.

———⊗⊗⊙———

Q. What Wild West entertainer buried three of his children in Rochester's Mount Hope Cemetery?

A. Buffalo Bill Cody.

———⊗⊗⊙———

Q. In what village can you attend "the Oldest Consecutive Rodeo East of the Mississippi" during the month of August?

A. Gerry, near Jamestown.

———⊗⊗⊙———

Q. At what event do pumpkins in excess of seven hundred pounds compete for the honor of "world's biggest"?

A. The World Pumpkin Weigh-Off, in Collins.

———⊗⊗⊙———

Q. Offering cruises to passengers since 1817, what is the oldest boat excursion company in the United States?

A. The Lake George Steamboat Company.

———⊗⊗⊙———

Q. What star of the TV series *The Rifleman* previously played pro basketball with the Rochester Royals?

A. Chuck Connors.

Q. Where was film star and sex symbol Mel Gibson born?

A. Peekskill.

Q. What star of the Oscar-winning film *Midnight Cowboy* was born in Yonkers on December 29, 1938?

A. Jon Voight.

Q. What 1991 gangster film starring Dustin Hoffman and Nicole Kidman was shot in the Saratoga Springs area?

A. *Billy Bathgate.*

HISTORY

C H A P T E R   T H R E E

Q. When did New York State enter the Union?

A. July 26, 1788.

Q. New York was what number state to ratify the Constitution and join the Union?

A. Eleventh.

Q. What famous manufacturer of cherry furniture is based in Syracuse?

A. L. & J. G. Stickley Company (founded in 1896).

Q. What signer of the Declaration of Independence was born in Brookhaven in 1727?

A. William Floyd.

Q. Where did President Benjamin Harrison have a summer camp?

A. On Second Lake, near Old Forge.

Q. What was President William McKinley's favorite summer vacation spot?

A. The Hotel Champlain, near Plattsburgh.

———

Q. What hunting club did Teddy Roosevelt often visit?

A. The Tahawus Club.

———

Q. Who dedicated the Whiteface Memorial Highway in 1935?

A. President Franklin D. Roosevelt.

———

Q. Who inspected Fort Ticonderoga near Lake George in 1783?

A. General George Washington.

———

Q. What war between the Americans and the British saw action on Lake Champlain?

A. The War of 1812.

———

Q. What was the first hotel in the world to have electric lights in all its guest rooms?

A. The Prospect House (1882–1903) in Blue Mountain Lake.

———

Q. One of the first important naval battles of the Revolutionary War was fought where?

A. Off Valcour Island in Lake Champlain (in the fall of 1776).

Q. Who was the most famous hermit in Adirondack history?

A. Noah John Rondeau, born in 1883.

———

Q. How many slaves were led to freedom by Auburn area resident Harriet Tubman through her "underground railroad"?

A. More than three hundred.

———

Q. In what town did Henry Wells, founder of Wells Fargo and American Express, begin his career as a shoemaker and mechanic?

A. Port Bryon.

———

Q. What city, founded by Colonel John Hardenburgh, was once the largest community in the state?

A. Auburn.

———

Q. Who made the first "Adirondack-style" chair?

A. Thomas Lee, of Westport (in 1903).

———

Q. What was the first railway to enter the Adirondacks?

A. The line from Saratoga to North Creek (built in 1871).

———

Q. Who founded the nation's first Red Cross chapter?

A. Clara Barton, in Livingston County (in 1881).

Q. How many times has New York City hosted the Republican National Convention?

A. None.

———⊗⊗⊗———

Q. How many times has New York City hosted the Democratic National Convention?

A. Five (1868, 1924, 1976, 1980, and 1992).

———⊗⊗⊗———

Q. What tragedy happened on July 17, 1996, off the south shore of Long Island?

A. TWA Flight 800 exploded in mid-air and crashed, killing all 230 aboard.

———⊗⊗⊗———

Q. What significant international anniversary was celebrated in New York City on October 22, 1995?

A. The fiftieth anniversary of the United Nations.

———⊗⊗⊗———

Q. New York City's Waldorf-Astoria hotel opened when?

A. 1897 (by John Jacob Astor).

———⊗⊗⊗———

Q. Who was the first vice president of the United States born in New York State?

A. George Clinton (born in Ulster County in 1739; served with Thomas Jefferson).

———⊗⊗⊗———

Q. When was the worst railroad disaster in New York State history?

A. November 1, 1918, in Brooklyn (ninety-seven deaths).

Q. What former first lady was born in Rye on June 8, 1925?

A. Barbara Bush.

Q. In what year did English explorer Henry Hudson sail into (what would become) New York Harbor?

A. 1609.

Q. Lake Champlain in the northeastern corner of New York State was named for whom?

A. Samuel de Champlain (who first explored the lake in 1609).

Q. When it was established as a Dutch province in 1624, what was the New York City area known as?

A. New Netherland.

Q. A railroad accident on November 22, 1950, that caused seventy-nine deaths occurred where in New York State?

A. Richmond Hill.

Q. Who helped Colonial troops capture Fort Ticonderoga on May 10, 1775?

A. Colonel Benedict Arnold.

Q. Fourteen people were killed when a U.S. Army B-25 crashed into what structure on July 28, 1945?

A. The Empire State Building, in New York City.

Q. What major battle did General George Washington and his ten thousand troops lose on August 27, 1776?

A. The Battle of Long Island.

Q. How long did it take for the first boat to make the trip from Buffalo to New York City on the Erie Canal?

A. Nine days (from October 26 to November 4, 1825).

Q. What religion was first organized on April 6, 1830, in Fayette by Joseph Smith?

A. Mormonism.

Q. What two women led the Women's Rights Convention in July 1848 in Seneca Falls?

A. Lucretia Mott and Elizabeth Cady Stanton.

Q. What famous retailer opened his first store in Utica on February 22, 1879?

A. F. W. Woolworth.

Q. When was the Statue of Liberty dedicated in New York Harbor?

A. October 28, 1886.

Q. What was the date of the World Trade Center bombing in New York City that resulted in six deaths?

A. February 26, 1993.

Q. What was the first permanent settlement of English-speaking people on Lake Champlain?

A. Skenesborough (established in 1761, where Whitehall is now).

—∞∞∞—

Q. British General John Burgoyne and his force of eight thousand troops captured what outpost on July 6, 1777?

A. Fort Ticonderoga.

—∞∞∞—

Q. Where did the first execution by electrocution in the United States take place?

A. Auburn Prison (on August 6, 1890).

—∞∞∞—

Q. When did Ellis Island in New York Harbor open as the primary immigration depot in the United States?

A. 1892.

—∞∞∞—

Q. The first transatlantic flight (with stops at Newfoundland, the Azores, and Lisbon) by a U.S. Navy seaplane left Rockaway on what date?

A. May 8, 1919.

—∞∞∞—

Q. Whom did Herbert Hoover defeat in the 1928 presidential election?

A. Alfred E. Smith (the governor of New York State).

—∞∞∞—

Q. When did the Empire State Building in New York City open?

A. May 1, 1931.

Q. Who was the first African-American woman elected to Congress?

A. Representative Shirley Chisholm (Democrat from New York City, elected in 1968).

———————

Q. In what upstate New York city was President William McKinley assassinated?

A. Buffalo (shot September 6, 1901; died September 14, 1901).

———————

Q. Who was the first woman ever nominated for U.S. vice president?

A. Geraldine Ferraro (Democratic U.S. representative from New York City, in 1984).

———————

Q. What merchant from Albany was one of the signers of the Declaration of Independence?

A. Phillip Livingston.

———————

Q. The inaugural and funeral trains of what U.S. president passed through Westchester County?

A. Abraham Lincoln.

———————

Q. Where is the birthplace of the U.S. Navy?

A. Whitehall (at the mouth of Lake Champlain).

———————

Q. What upstate New York museum offers a "real-life" historical perspective on nineteenth-century New York State?

A. Genesee Country Village and Museum, in Mumford.

Q. In what year was the city of Buffalo chartered?

A. 1832.

Q. In 1872, who became the first American woman to vote in a presidential election (and was arrested for doing so)?

A. Susan B. Anthony, in Rochester.

Q. What was the first Episcopal Cathedral in America?

A. The Cathedral of All Saints in Albany (begun 1884, still unfinished).

Q. What defeat of British troops led by General Burgoyne became known as the turning point of the Revolutionary War?

A. The Battles of Saratoga (October 1777).

Q. When and where was New York State's first fair held?

A. In 1819 on the lawn of the Capitol in Albany.

Q. What was America's first passenger railroad?

A. The Dewitt Clinton, between Albany and Schenectady (1831).

Q. What upstate New York mayor served his city for forty-one years, from 1942 to 1983?

A. Erastus Corning II, of Albany.

Q. In what year was the University of Buffalo established?

A. 1846.

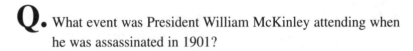

Q. What event was President William McKinley attending when he was assassinated in 1901?

A. The Pan American Exposition.

Q. What former mayor of Buffalo would go on to become the president of the United States?

A. Grover Cleveland (served as mayor in 1882).

Q. In what year did the Saint Lawrence Seaway open?

A. 1959.

Q. For whom is the city of Rochester named?

A. Soldier and landowner Nathaniel Rochester.

Q. When did Dutch settlers first establish farms on Long Island?

A. 1624.

Q. In what year did the Long Island Railroad incorporate?

A. 1834.

Q. What was the first state capital of New York?

A. Kingston.

———⊗⊗⊘———

Q. Where was Franklin D. Roosevelt born in 1882?

A. Hyde Park.

———⊗⊗⊘———

Q. When was Vassar College in Poughkeepsie incorporated?

A. 1861.

———⊗⊗⊘———

Q. On what date did Italian explorer Giovanni da Verrazano enter (what would become) New York Harbor?

A. April 17, 1524.

———⊗⊗⊘———

Q. In what year did the five tribes of the Iroquois—the Mohawk, Oneida, Onondaga, Cayuga, and Seneca—found the League of Five Nations?

A. 1570.

———⊗⊗⊘———

Q. What was Henry Hudson looking for in 1609 when he sailed his ship the *Half Moon* into New York Bay?

A. A passage to China.

———⊗⊗⊘———

Q. Who was the first Jewish settler to arrive in New York?

A. Jacob Barsimon (on July 8, 1654).

Q. On what date was the city of New Amsterdam surrendered by the Dutch to the British, thus becoming New York?

A. September 9, 1664.

Q. In what year did the French build a fort at Crown Point?

A. 1731.

Q. Who captured Fort Ticonderoga on May 10, 1775?

A. Ethan Allen and the Green Mountain Boys.

Q. What did the Provincial Congress ratify on July 9, 1776, at White Plains?

A. The Declaration of Independence.

Q. In what city did Theodore Roosevelt take the oath of office for the U.S. presidency?

A. Buffalo (in 1901, after McKinley's assassination).

Q. Who purchased Staten Island from Native Americans in 1668?

A. Francis Lovelace (the second British governor).

Q. Who was executed on Long Island by the British for espionage on September 22, 1776?

A. Nathan Hale.

Q. What battle did General George Washington and his troops lose on October 28, 1776?

A. The Battle of White Plains.

———— ∞ ————

Q. While Auburn resident William Seward was secretary of state under Andrew Johnson, what purchase did he recommend that became known as "Seward's Folly"?

A. The 1867 purchase of the Alaskan territory.

———— ∞ ————

Q. Where was the first state constitution adopted?

A. Kingston (on April 20, 1777).

———— ∞ ————

Q. Who was the first governor of New York State?

A. George Clinton (inaugurated July 9, 1777).

———— ∞ ————

Q. On October 17, 1777, what British officer surrendered his troops at Schuylerville (Old Saratoga)?

A. Major General John Burgoyne.

———— ∞ ————

Q. On what date did Anthony Wayne's colonial troops capture Stony Point, thereby establishing control over the lower Hudson Valley?

A. July 16, 1779.

———— ∞ ————

Q. Where was the last battle to take place in New York State during the Revolutionary War?

A. At Johnstown (on October 25, 1781).

Q. The British finally evacuated Manhattan on what date?

A. November 25, 1783.

———✸———

Q. What institution did Governor George Clinton establish on May 1, 1784?

A. The State University of New York.

———✸———

Q. In what year was Fort Niagara built?

A. 1679.

———✸———

Q. The American Bar Association was formed in what upstate community in 1878?

A. Saratoga Springs.

———✸———

Q. Where was George Washington inaugurated as the first American president on April 30, 1789?

A. The steps of Federal Hall in Manhattan.

———✸———

Q. Albany become the capital of New York State in what year?

A. 1797.

———✸———

Q. What was founded at West Point on March 16, 1802?

A. The United States Military Academy.

Q. A Dutch trading post built near Albany in 1614 was given what name?

A. Fort Nassau.

Q. British troops raided Ogdensburg in northern New York State in what year?

A. 1813.

Q. On what date did the Americans defeat the British in the Battle of Lake Champlain?

A. September 11, 1814.

Q. With whom did the Iroquois League of Five Nations form an alliance in 1684?

A. The British.

Q. Who founded the first women's college in the United States?

A. Emma Willard (Troy Female Seminary, in 1821).

Q. In what year did Joseph Smith have revelations near Palmyra that led to the founding of the Mormon religion?

A. 1823.

Q. How many people were freed when New York State abolished slavery on July 4, 1827?

A. Approximately ten thousand.

Q. The first Women's Rights Convention was held in what town on July 19, 1848?

A. Seneca Falls.

―――⊗⊗⊗―――

Q. In 1862, how many regiments did the state send to the Civil War?

A. 120.

―――⊗⊗⊗―――

Q. What was the original name of the institution founded in 1754, and later renamed Columbia University?

A. King's College.

―――⊗⊗⊗―――

Q. In what year were women granted suffrage in state elections?

A. 1917.

―――⊗⊗⊗―――

Q. What group of people established New Rochelle in 1688?

A. Huguenot settlers.

―――⊗⊗⊗―――

Q. Who were the first women in New York State elected to the state legislature?

A. Mary M. Lilly and Ida B. Sammis Get, in 1919.

―――⊗⊗⊗―――

Q. From what airport did Charles Lindbergh begin his historic nonstop flight across the Atlantic Ocean on May 20, 1927?

A. Roosevelt Airport, on Long Island.

Q. Amsterdam merchant Kiliaen van Rensselaer founded what area in 1630?

A. Rensselaerswyck (now Albany, Rensselaer, and Columbia counties).

———∞∞———

Q. In what year did former New York Governor Franklin Roosevelt first get elected president of the United States?

A. 1932.

———∞∞———

Q. Construction of the New York State Thruway was authorized in what year?

A. 1950.

———∞∞———

Q. The state lottery was legalized in what year?

A. 1966.

———∞∞———

Q. Who was the second governor of New York State?

A. John Jay (from 1795 to 1801).

———∞∞———

Q. What leader of English and Dutch frontiersmen led the defeat of the French and Native Americans in the Battle of La Prairie in 1690?

A. Peter Schuyler (mayor of Albany).

———∞∞———

Q. When was William Marcy, Mount Marcy's namesake, governor of New York?

A. 1833–1838.

Q. In what year did the first Saint Patrick's Day parade take place in New York City?

A. 1762.

Q. How many members of the Whig Party served as governor of New York State (all in the mid-1800s)?

A. Four (William Seward, John Young, Hamilton Fish, and Myron Clark).

Q. In what years has New York State had constitutional conventions?

A. 1777, 1822, 1846, and 1894.

Q. What is the highest court in New York State?

A. The court of appeals.

Q. In what years did Nelson Rockefeller serve as governor of New York State?

A. 1959–1973.

Q. What does the term *knickerbocker* refer to?

A. The wide breeches worn by early Dutch settlers.

Q. Where was the first school in America organized?

A. In New Amsterdam (1633).

Q. How many years did it take to build the State Capitol building?

A. Thirty-one (1867–1898).

———— ∞ ————

Q. In what year did English explorer Sebastian Cabot chart waters along the latitude and longitude of New York?

A. 1497.

———— ∞ ————

Q. What name did Spanish explorer Gomez give to the river we know as the Hudson?

A. San Antonio.

———— ∞ ————

Q. How many times was DeWitt Clinton governor of New York?

A. Twice (1817–1822 and 1825–1828).

———— ∞ ————

Q. What was the city of Rome originally known as when first settled in 1786?

A. Lynchville.

———— ∞ ————

Q. The American flag first flew over Fort Ontario at Oswego in 1796 on the shores of what Great Lake?

A. Ontario.

———— ∞ ————

Q. What institution of higher learning was chartered during the War of 1812?

A. Hamilton College.

Q. In what year did Martin Van Buren serve as governor of New York?

A. 1829.

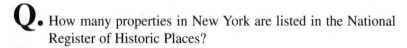

Q. How many properties in New York are listed in the National Register of Historic Places?

A. Nearly sixty-two thousand.

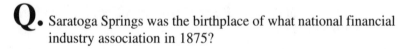

Q. What was the first state historic site in America?

A. Washington's Headquarters, in Newburgh.

Q. In 1901, New York became the first state to require what adornments for automobiles?

A. License plates.

Q. Saratoga Springs was the birthplace of what national financial industry association in 1875?

A. The American Bankers Association.

Q. What first-of-its-kind transportation system began operating on October 27, 1904?

A. The New York City subway system.

Q. In what year did the Empire State Plaza open in Albany?

A. 1978.

Q. Who won the gubernatorial election by the biggest landslide in state history?

A. Mario Cuomo (in 1986, for his second term).

———⊗⊗⊗———

Q. Who was the most recent governor of New York to win his national party's nomination for president?

A. Thomas E. Dewey (in 1948, lost to Truman).

———⊗⊗⊗———

Q. In what year did Ann Lee and the Shaker Mission arrive in New York from England?

A. 1774.

———⊗⊗⊗———

Q. What company that would one day urge travelers, "Don't leave home without it," was founded in Albany in 1841?

A. The American Express Company.

———⊗⊗⊗———

Q. Who was the first president in American history to have been born a U.S. citizen?

A. Martin Van Buren (born in Kinderhook on December 5, 1782).

———⊗⊗⊗———

Q. Where was the first hard-surfaced road in America?

A. From Kingston running south about one hundred miles into northern New Jersey (1663).

———⊗⊗⊗———

Q. What was the name of the Adirondack Great Camp first owned by William West Durant in 1876 and later sold to Collis Huntington, builder of the Southern Pacific Railroad?

A. Camp Pine Knot.

Q. What governor owned Echo Camp, on Raquette Lake, after it was built in 1883?

A. Governor Phinneas Lounsbury (of Connecticut!).

———⊗⊗⊗———

Q. What historic lighthouse was built at the mouth of the Genesee River at Lake Ontario?

A. The Charlotte Lighthouse.

———⊗⊗⊗———

Q. What 150-year-old farm in western New York is now a family attraction for its berry picking and petting zoo, and once served as a stop for the Underground Railroad?

A. Murphy Orchards, in Burt.

———⊗⊗⊗———

Q. The state historic site at Ganondagan near Victor was known as what from 1650 to 1687?

A. The "capital" of the Seneca Indian Nation.

———⊗⊗⊗———

Q. What canal town had the distinction in the mid-1800s of being an international exporter of peppermint?

A. Lyons.

———⊗⊗⊗———

Q. The New York State Historical Association is based in what town?

A. Cooperstown.

———⊗⊗⊗———

Q. In what upstate community was the American Historical Association founded?

A. Saratoga Springs (September 10, 1884).

Q. When he was a twenty-three-year-old freshman assemblyman in Albany (1882), Theodore Roosevelt earned what nickname for his aggressiveness?

A. The Cyclone Assemblyman.

Q. What did Governor Alfred Smith install in the backyard of the Executive Mansion during his three terms?

A. A zoo with elk, monkeys, bears, and a goat named Heliotrope.

Q. What tiny Lake Ontario port community developed into a major military and naval operations complex during the War of 1812?

A. Sackets Harbor.

Q. The brother and sister of what famous European leader lived in Cape Vincent in the Thousand Islands area for a time?

A. Napoleon Bonaparte.

Q. In 1980, what activist turned himself in to authorities after living on Wellesley Island in the Saint Lawrence River for years under the name Barry Freed?

A. Abbie Hoffman.

Q. What former U.S. president and resident of East Aurora was credited with delaying the start of the Civil War by ten years with his Compromise of 1850?

A. Millard Fillmore.

Q. What was the original name of Fort Ticonderoga?

A. Fort Carillon.

———— ∞ ————

Q. Who was governor of New York from 1955 to 1958?

A. Averill Harriman.

———— ∞ ————

Q. Who captured Fort William Henry in 1757 for the French?

A. General Marquis de Montcalm.

———— ∞ ————

Q. New York State's boundaries were finally settled in what year?

A. 1881 (after a long dispute with Connecticut).

———— ∞ ————

Q. Where is the resting place of the *Land Tortoise*, one of America's oldest warships?

A. At the bottom of Lake George (one hundred feet down).

———— ∞ ————

Q. What mountain was Vice President Teddy Roosevelt climbing when informed that President William McKinley was dying of his gunshot wound in Buffalo?

A. Mount Marcy.

———— ∞ ————

Q. In what year did the Executive Mansion in Albany become the home for governors of New York?

A. 1874.

Q. How many original counties were there in New York?

A. Ten (all founded on November 1, 1683).

———✖———

Q. What was the last county to be established in New York State?

A. Bronx County (founded January 1, 1914).

———✖———

Q. What "marriage" ended in divorce in 1689?

A. The Dominion of New England (which had been the 1686 union of New York and New England).

———✖———

Q. What settlement was massacred by French and Indian troops in 1690?

A. Schenectady.

———✖———

Q. In what year was the Brooklyn Bridge opened?

A. 1883.

———✖———

Q. Alfred E. Smith was reelected governor how many times?

A. Three (the last time in 1924).

———✖———

Q. Temporary headquarters for the newly formed United Nations were set up where in 1945?

A. Lake Success.

Q. Julius and Ethel Rosenberg were convicted and executed as spies in 1951 at what facility?

A. Sing Sing Prison.

Q. Who was the British general famous for his ill-fated attack on Fort Ticonderoga in 1758?

A. James Abercrombie.

Q. Who was the feminist and reformer, born in Homer in 1818, who had an article of women's clothing named for her?

A. Amelia Jenks Bloomer.

Q. What famous abolitionist born in 1800 lived for a period of his life in the Adirondacks?

A. John Brown.

Q. William George Fargo, the founder of the American Express Company, held what political office from 1862 to 1866?

A. Mayor of Buffalo.

Q. In what town was famous capitalist John D. Rockefeller born?

A. Richford (in 1839).

Q. On the site of what fort was Utica settled in 1773?

A. Fort Schuyler.

Q. While he was governor, Theodore Roosevelt converted space on the third floor of the Executive Mansion for what purpose?

A. To build a boxing gymnasium.

———&<——

Q. What was discovered at the bottom of Lake Champlain in June 1997?

A. One of Benedict Arnold's warships.

———&<——

Q. A shipyard in what Washington County town was the first for the U.S. Navy?

A. Whitehall (early 1800s).

———&<——

Q. At what museum can you see a lock of George Washington's hair, Ethan Allen's pocket compass, and a rum horn given to General Schuyler by Paul Revere?

A. Fort Ticonderoga.

———&<——

Q. After completing a trip around the world, who called Skaneateles Lake near Syracuse "the most beautiful body of water in the world"?

A. William H. Seward (secretary of state under Abraham Lincoln).

———&<——

Q. Who was responsible for persuading Abraham Lincoln in a letter that he would look better if he grew a beard during the 1860 presidential campaign?

A. Eleven-year-old Grace Bedell, of Westfield (he later thanked her).

Q. Once known to the Iroquois as the "medicine springs of the Great Spirit," what mineral spring was visited in 1771 by Sir William Johnson?

A. High Rock Spring, in Saratoga Springs.

Q. What nephew of Alexander Hamilton founded the town of Angelica in 1800?

A. Captain Phillip Church.

Q. In what town was feminist and reformer Elizabeth Cady Stanton born in 1815?

A. Johnstown.

Q. Who was the American naval commander who successfully defeated the British on September 11, 1814, on Lake Champlain?

A. Commodore Thomas Macdonough.

Q. Who was known as the founder of Saratoga Springs and now has a famous resort hotel named for him?

A. Gideon Putnam.

ARTS & LITERATURE

CHAPTER FOUR

Q. Theodore Dreiser wrote what novel based on the 1906 murder of Grace Brown by Chester Gillete, which occurred at Big Moose in the Adirondacks?

A. *An American Tragedy.*

Q. What repertory theater group makes its home in Endicott?

A. The Cider Mill Playhouse.

Q. What artist and journalist, along with Ralph Waldo Emerson, formed the Adirondack Club for philosophers and writers?

A. William J. Stillman (in August 1858).

Q. University of Rochester alum Francis Bellamy wrote what familiar patriotic passage?

A. The Pledge of Allegiance (in 1892).

Q. Curt Smith, a 1973 graduate of the State University College at Geneseo, wrote what book related to baseball?

A. *Voices of the Game* (a history of baseball broadcasting).

Q. Who wrote the phrase "Yes, Virginia, there is a Santa Claus"?

A. *New York Sun* editor Francis Church (in 1897, in response to a letter from eight-year-old Virginia O'Hanlon).

Q. What New York City–based magazine ceased weekly publication after thirty-six years in 1972?

A. *Life*.

Q. Born on a farm in Greenwich in 1860, painter Anna Mary Robertson Moses better known by what name?

A. Grandma Moses.

Q. Who cofounded the New York City Ballet in 1948?

A. Lincoln Kirstein.

Q. What is the longest-running Broadway musical in history?

A. *Cats* (more than 6,150 performances).

Q. What book by New York author James Fenimore Cooper is often regarded as the first historical novel in America?

A. *The Spy* (written in 1821).

Q. What is the name of the nonprofit professional theater company based in Rochester?

A. GeVa Theatre.

Q. What is the thirty-seventh-largest newspaper in the United States?

A. *The Buffalo News* (1995 circulation of 274,614).

Q. What outdoor amphitheater serves as the summer home of the New York City Ballet and the Philadelphia Orchestra?

A. The Saratoga Performing Arts Center, in Saratoga Springs.

Q. Who won a Pulitzer Prize in 1997 for the novel *Martin Dressler: The Tale of an American Dreamer*?

A. Steven Millhauser (a professor at Skidmore College, in Saratoga Springs).

Q. As of 1997, how many times had *Newsday*, the Long Island-based daily newspaper, won the Pulitzer Prize for meritorious public service?

A. Twice (1954 and 1970).

Q. What is the largest symphony orchestra in New York's "Southern Tier"?

A. The Binghamton Symphony Orchestra.

Q. Who wrote *Nobody's Fool*, the novel about upstate life in a depressed town that became a film starring Paul Newman?

A. Richard Russo.

Q. Robert Louis Stevenson completed what book while he was a tuberculosis patient in Saranac Lake?

A. *Master of Ballantrae.*

Q. In Sylvia Plath's novel *The Bell Jar*, where did her skiing accident take place?

A. At Mount Pisgah, in Saranac Lake.

Q. Where was mystery writer Joyce Carol Oates born?

A. Lockport.

Q. Where was the first home for the Museum of Cartoon Art?

A. Westchester County.

Q. What famous nineteenth-century author lived for a time in Mamaroneck and Scarsdale?

A. James Fenimore Cooper.

Q. In what town was Frederic Remington, a famous painter of Old West scenes, born in 1861?

A. Canton.

Q. Croton-on-Hudson resident and author Roger Kahn wrote what classic baseball book?

A. *The Boys of Summer.*

Q. What upstate New York daily newspaper won the 1959 Pulitzer Prize for meritorious public service?

A. *Utica Observer-Dispatch.*

Q. What notable opera company makes its home at the Onondaga County Civic Center?

A. The Syracuse Opera.

Q. Washington Irving, author of *The Legend of Sleepy Hollow*, lived in what community?

A. Tarrytown.

Q. The Anderson Center for the Arts, host to international performing artists, is located where?

A. On the campus of SUNY-Binghamton.

Q. Archie, Jughead, and their friends come to life on pages published in what town?

A. Mamaroneck.

Q. Where was *Charlotte's Web* author E. B. White born?

A. Mount Vernon.

Q. What writer for a small Finger Lakes area newspaper won a Pulitzer Prize for reporting in 1930?

A. W. O. Dappin (of the *Auburn Citizen*).

Q. What is the fifty-ninth-largest newspaper in the nation?

A. The Rochester *Democrat & Chronicle* (1995 circulation of 194,677).

Q. Where is composer Sergei Rachmaninoff buried?

A. Kensico Cemetery, in Westchester County.

———∞———

Q. Where are the corporate headquarters for *The Reader's Digest*?

A. Chappaqua, in the town of New Castle.

———∞———

Q. Where are the Donald M. Kendall Sculpture Gardens located?

A. At the PepsiCo world headquarters in Purchase.

———∞———

Q. *The Pioneers*, a novel written by James Fenimore Cooper and published in 1823, was about the settlement of what community?

A. Cooperstown.

———∞———

Q. What syndicated cartoonist and creator of the strip *B.C.* makes his home in Broome County?

A. Johnny Hart.

———∞———

Q. What national newspaper was founded by the Gannett Corporation, formerly based in Rochester?

A. *USA Today*.

———∞———

Q. Ian Fleming's *The Spy Who Loved Me* is set partially in what resort area?

A. Lake George.

Q. Where did Norman Rockwell go to high school?

A. Mamaroneck High School, in Westchester County.

———⊗∞⊘———

Q. Who was the Sarah Lawrence College graduate who wrote *The Color Purple*?

A. Alice Walker.

———⊗∞⊘———

Q. The thirty-one-hundred-seat Eastman Theater in Rochester is part of what music school?

A. The Eastman School of Music.

———⊗∞⊘———

Q. What author, whose works included *Lassie*, made his home in Croton-on-Hudson?

A. Eric Knight.

———⊗∞⊘———

Q. What native of Albany won the Pulitzer Prize for fiction in 1984?

A. William Kennedy (for *Ironweed*).

———⊗∞⊘———

Q. What is one of the few remaining free-admission outdoor Shakespeare festivals in the nation?

A. Buffalo's Shakespeare in the Park series.

———⊗∞⊘———

Q. How many art galleries are there in New York City?

A. More than four hundred.

Q. What museum has the largest collection of Egyptian antiquities outside of London or Cairo?

A. The Brooklyn Museum.

Q. What museum has the largest collection of Iroquois artifacts in the world?

A. The Rochester Museum & Science Center.

Q. What was the first newspaper in New York?

A. *The New York Gazette*, first published on October 16, 1725.

Q. In what year was *The Legend of Sleepy Hollow* author Washington Irving born?

A. 1783 (April 3).

Q. In what year did painter Thomas Cole establish the Hudson River School, America's first major school of painting?

A. 1825.

Q. In the artwork on the state seal, what two figures appear?

A. The goddess of liberty and the goddess of justice.

Q. What is the only state park in the nation dedicated entirely to the visual and performing arts?

A. Artpark in Lewiston (near Niagara Falls).

Q. Where can you find the largest collection of sheet music in the world?

A. The Sibley Music Library, at the Eastman School of Music in Rochester.

Q. What Pulitzer Prize–winning syndicated columnist was born in Mount Vernon on October 20, 1925?

A. Art Buchwald.

Q. What is the name of the nonprofit professional theater company based in Buffalo?

A. Studio Arena Theatre.

Q. What was the name of the newspaper first published by Alexander Hamilton on October 27, 1787?

A. *The Federalist.*

Q. What landscape painter of upstate scenes was born in 1847 and had his work ignored until late in his life, after he was committed to an asylum for the insane?

A. Ralph Albert Blakelock.

Q. The New York Library Association, the first state library society in America, was formed in what year?

A. 1890 (in Albany).

Q. The verses to "Yankee Doodle" were written by whom and in what year?

A. Dr. Richard Shuckburgh in 1755 (in Albany).

Q. What 1944 book was about the life of a doctor in Palmyra during the building of the Erie Canal?

A. *Canal Town* (by Samuel H. Adams).

Q. Where was David Malkowich, an author of espionage thrillers, born?

A. Amsterdam.

Q. What upstate New York community is home to the renowned Garth Fagan Dance Company?

A. Rochester.

Q. In what year was James Fenimore Cooper's classic novel *The Last of the Mohicans* published?

A. 1826.

Q. Who wrote the 1987 novel *World's End*, which chronicled the lives of several generations of a Hudson Valley family?

A. T. Coraghessan Boyle.

Q. What photographer is known for his scenes of the Adirondack region?

A. Nathan Farb.

Q. How many museums are there in New York City?

A. More than 150.

Q. What famous political cartoonist was born in Saranac Lake?

A. Garry Trudeau (creator of *Doonesbury*).

Q. Where is the Tri-Cities Opera company based?

A. Binghamton.

Q. Where was syndicated cartoonist John McPherson (*Close to Home*) born?

A. Painted Post.

Q. Who wrote *Brother to the Enemy*, the 1958 historical novel about Benedict Arnold?

A. Bart Spicer.

Q. What 1986 novel by Richard Russo was set in the cities of Gloversville and Johnstown?

A. *Mohawk*.

Q. Who wrote the 1988 nonfiction book about Long Island fishermen *Men's Lives: The Surfmen and Baymen of South Fork*?

A. Peter Matthiessen.

Q. Washington Irving's stories "Rip Van Winkle" and "The Legend of Sleepy Hollow," regionalized to the Hudson Valley, were based on what?

A. German folktales.

Q. Who is the editor of *Adirondack Life* and author of *The Adirondack Book*?

A. Elizabeth Folwell.

Q. At what upstate museum can be found one of the world's premier collections of photographs, films, and rare books?

A. The International Museum of Photography, at the George Eastman House in Rochester.

Q. What syndicated columnist and national cynic was born in Albany on January 14, 1919?

A. Andy Rooney.

Q. What arts festival annually draws a half million people and celebrated its fortieth anniversary in 1997?

A. The Allentown Art Festival, in Buffalo.

Q. Who wrote the romantic novel *Saratoga Trunk* in 1941?

A. Edna Ferber.

Q. Where was poet Ogden Nash born and raised?

A. Rye.

Q. *The Wasp*, the first comic magazine in America, was published where in 1802?

A. Hudson.

Q. What upstate New York-based editorial cartoonist won a Pulitzer Prize in 1990?

A. Tom Toles (of the *Buffalo News*).

———❀———

Q. Who wrote the 1954 novel *Blessed Is the Land*, about the first Jewish immigrants to New Amsterdam in 1654?

A. Louis Zara.

———❀———

Q. What Rochester daily afternoon newspaper ceased publication on June 27, 1997, after seventy-four years?

A. The *Times-Union*.

———❀———

Q. Ismail Merchant and James Ivory, the film production team famous for such period films as *Remains of the Day* and *Howard's End*, live in what county?

A. Columbia.

———❀———

Q. What art gallery is set in one of the oldest buildings in Claverlack, Columbia County, and operated by the Merchant-Ivory Foundation?

A. Red Mills Gallery.

———❀———

Q. Which of the fifty largest orchestras in the nation makes its home in the Eastman Theatre?

A. The Rochester Philharmonic.

Q. What is one of the only museums in the nation where you can take workshops on wooden boatbuilding and rustic furniture making?

A. The Adirondack Museum, in Blue Mountain Lake.

Q. What 1953 novel by John Brick was based on the life of upstate Revolutionary War hero Timothy Murphy?

A. *The Rifleman.*

Q. What is the home of the Buffalo Philharmonic Orchestra?

A. Kleinhans Music Hall.

Q. What magazine publisher owned Bluff Point, an Adirondack Great Camp built on Raquette Lake in 1877?

A. Robert Collier (*Collier's*).

Q. What is the second-largest theater stage in the state?

A. The stage at Artpark, in Lewiston.

Q. The work of how many American craftsmen are on display at Artisans Alley in Niagara Falls?

A. More than six hundred.

Q. What was the name of the newspaper published by abolitionist Frederick Douglass in Rochester?

A. *The North Star.*

Q. At what museum will you find more than four hundred paintings and sculptures of sport hunting and wildlife?

A. The Gallery of Sporting Art, in Mumford.

Q. What satirical novel about New York high society was written in 1987 by Tom Wolfe?

A. *The Bonfire of the Vanities.*

Q. What internationally acclaimed opera festival takes place along the shores of Otsego Lake?

A. The Glimmerglass Opera.

Q. The film adaptation of Henry James's *Portrait of a Lady* starred Nicole Kidman, who played a character based on whom?

A. James's Albany cousin, Mary Temple.

Q. Martha Gellhorn, who married Ernest Hemingway, once worked for what upstate newspaper?

A. The Albany *Times-Union.*

Q. In what community did Mark Twain write *The Adventures of Huckleberry Finn*?

A. Elmira.

Q. At what art museum will you find the largest collection of American West art east of the Mississippi?

A. At the Rockwell Museum, in Corning.

Q. Who founded the Roycroft Movement at East Aurora in 1895, a complex that attracted hundreds of artisans and famous visitors such as Henry Ford and Thomas Edison?

A. Elbert Hubbard.

Q. How many people can be seated in the performance amphitheater at Chautauqua?

A. Six thousand.

Q. More than ninety-five hundred works of art are included in the permanent collection of what gallery in Rochester?

A. Memorial Art Gallery.

Q. What artist and gallery owner in Washington County has a very famous great-grandmother?

A. Will Moses (great-grandson of Grandma Moses).

Q. In what "middle of nowhere" location can you find an arts center that offers more than 120 concerts, workshops, and exhibits on a year-round basis?

A. The Adirondack Lakes Center for the Arts, in Blue Mountain Lake.

Q. What noted author came to Saranac Lake during the winter of 1887–88 in an attempt to restore his failing health?

A. Robert Louis Stevenson.

Q. Where did writer William F. Buckley once travel to christen the new peanut roaster of the company that made his favorite peanut butter?

A. The Red Wing Foods Company, in Fredonia.

Q. *Bullet Park* by John Cheever was a 1969 satirical novel about a family from what county?

A. Westchester.

Q. Where is Palestine Park, a 350-foot-long model of the Holy Land used to teach biblical geography?

A. At Chautauqua, on Lake Chautauqua.

Q. What Buffalo museum is renowned for its contemporary art collection?

A. The Albright-Knox Art Gallery.

Q. In what town is the Crane School of Music located?

A. Potsdam.

Q. What 1869 book led to the emergence of the Adirondacks as a tourism and recreational area?

A. *Adirondacks in the Wilderness* (by William H. H. Murray).

Q. In what city did Mark Twain get married after meeting his future wife Olivia there on a visit?

A. Elmira.

Q. What is the name of the professional equity theater company in Albany?

A. Capital Repertory Company.

Q. Hubbard Hall in Cambridge, now an artisans center, served what purpose in the nineteenth century?

A. It was an opera house.

Q. The Empire State Ballet is based in what city?

A. Buffalo.

Q. Who wrote *Drums Along the Mohawk*, a 1936 novel about the Mohawk Valley and set during the American Revolution?

A. Walter D. Edmonds.

Q. What small western New York community boasts both a ballet and an opera company within its area?

A. Jamestown (Chautauqua Opera and the Chautauqua Ballet Company).

Q. Where is the Parrish Art Museum located?

A. Long Island.

Q. Who wrote the 1920 novel *The Age of Innocence*, which dealt with the wealthy New York society of the 1870s?

A. Edith Wharton.

Q. In what city is the Everson Museum of Art located?

A. Syracuse.

Q. What writer and poet, born in Roxbury in 1837, was known as the founder of the nature essay?

A. John Burroughs.

Q. What author and women's right advocate attended Vassar College and won the Pulitzer Prize in 1922 for her novel *Figs from Thistles*?

A. Edna Saint Vincent Millay.

Q. What is the origin of the name *Yaddo* given to a renowned writer's retreat in Saratoga Springs?

A. The daughter of the original owners, the Trask family, would say "yaddo" instead of "shadow."

Q. What Adirondack Great Camp and former summer retreat of the Alfred G. Vanderbilt family now serves as an attraction and arts center open to the public?

A. Great Camp Sagamore.

Q. What award-winning equine photographer resides in Saratoga Springs?

A. Barbara Livingston.

Q. Artist Jenness Cortez of Averill Park is known for her scenes of what famous sports setting?

A. Horse racing at the historic Saratoga Race Course.

Q. What humorist and journalist, born in 1881, went by the initials "F. P. A.," and wrote for several New York City newspapers during the early 1900s?

A. Franklin Pierce Adams.

Q. What noted art museum is located in Elmira?

A. The Arnot Art Museum.

Q. What Academy Award–winning film was based on Dunkirk-born author Samuel Hopkins Adams's novelette *Night Bus*?

A. *It Happened One Night.*

Q. What well-known 1980 E. L. Doctorow novel was set in the Adirondacks?

A. *Loon Lake.*

Q. The work of what *New Yorker* magazine cartoonist inspired the TV comedy series *The Addams Family*?

A. Charles Samuel Addams.

Q. What highly regarded art museum is located in Utica?

A. Munson-Williams-Proctor Museum.

Q. What naturalist and sculptor was born in Orleans County in 1864 and made the first film of gorillas in their natural habitat in 1921?

A. Carl Ethan Akeley.

Q. Where does the Rochester Philharmonic Orchestra make its summer home?

A. At the Finger Lakes Performing Arts Center, in Canandaigua.

Q. Best known for his western landscapes, what artist was born in 1830 and maintained a studio in Irvington?

A. Albert Bierstadt.

Q. What famous author and illustrator of children's books once worked for the New York City advertising agency McCann-Erickson?

A. Theodor Geisel Seuss (Dr. Seuss).

Q. What poet, author, and editor was born in Fort Hamilton in 1886?

A. William Rose Benet.

Q. According to the *Places Rated Almanac*, what western New York city has the second-highest reading quotient in the United States?

A. Jamestown.

Q. What 1898 novel by Edward Westcott told the story of a Syracuse banker during the Civil War?

A. *David Harum: A Story of an American Life*.

Q. What photographer, famed for his Civil War photographs taken at Bull Run and Gettysburg, was born in Warren County around 1823?

A. Matthew B. Brady.

Q. What painter and inventor helped found Vassar College in 1861 and was known for his landscapes of upstate New York?

A. Samuel Morse.

Q. What prominent landscape artist of the nineteenth century was known for his 1869 impression of Lake George?

A. John Frederick Kensett.

SPORTS & LEISURE

C H A P T E R   F I V E

Q. How many National Football League teams play their games in New York State?

A. One (Buffalo Bills).

Q. What three NBA franchises were based in upstate New York?

A. Buffalo Braves, Rochester Royals, and the Syracuse Nationals.

Q. Where is New York State's only ski gondola lift?

A. At Gore Mountain, in North Creek.

Q. What shopping center is regarded as the first enclosed urban mall in America?

A. Midtown Plaza in Rochester.

Q. What is the only community in New York State to have ever hosted the Olympic Games?

A. Lake Placid (the Winter Games in 1932 and 1980).

Q. What long-time head of ABC Sports was born in Forest Hills?

A. Roone Arledge.

Q. What special event held annually in Endicott celebrates both a sandwich and hot-air balloons?

A. The Spiedie Fest and Balloon Rally.

Q. How many National Hockey League teams play their games in New York State?

A. Three (Buffalo Sabres, New York Islanders, and New York Rangers).

Q. What is the seating capacity of Madison Square Garden, home of the New York Knicks and New York Rangers?

A. 19,694.

Q. In what years did the Buffalo Bills win the championship of the old American Football League?

A. 1964 and 1965.

Q. What mountain was the site of the 1980 Winter Olympic alpine skiing competition?

A. Whiteface Mountain, near Lake Placid.

Q. The world-record summer flounder was caught where?

A. Off the coast of Montauk on Long Island (twenty-two pounds, seven ounces).

Q. What ski area in western New York has the greatest vertical drop for mountains situated between the Adirondacks and the Rockies?

A. Bristol Mountain (twelve hundred feet).

Q. Where is the National Motor Racing Museum & Hall of Fame located?

A. Watkins Glen.

Q. What is known as the Carousel Capital of the World and features six restored wood-carved merry-go-rounds?

A. Broome County.

Q. On what western New York course did Paul Runyan win the 1934 PGA Championship over New Yorker Craig Wood?

A. Park Country Club, in Williamsville.

Q. Where is the National Museum of Racing & Hall of Fame located?

A. Saratoga Springs.

Q. Where is the Hall of Fame of the Trotter located?

A. Goshen.

Q. Where was the first ski lift in New York State?

A. The rope tow at the North Creek Ski Bowl (1934).

Q. The bobsled and luge competitions for the 1980 Winter Olympics were held on what mountain?

A. Mount Van Hoevenberg, near Lake Placid.

———— ∞ ————

Q. How many times did professional golfer Walter Hagen of Rochester win the PGA Championship?

A. Five (1921, and 1924–1927).

———— ∞ ————

Q. What was once one of the biggest high school football stadiums in the United States?

A. Aquinas (later Holleder) Stadium in Rochester (twenty thousand seats).

———— ∞ ————

Q. What is the capacity of the Arena at the Rochester War Memorial (since its 1997 expansion)?

A. Twelve thousand (up from seventy-three hundred).

———— ∞ ————

Q. In what Adirondack town did boxers Gene Tunney, Max Baer, and Max Schmeling train during the 1920s and 1930s?

A. Speculator.

———— ∞ ————

Q. How many times has Winged Foot Country Club in Mamaroneck hosted the U.S. Open Golf Championship?

A. Four (1929, 1959, 1974, and 1984).

———— ∞ ————

Q. The first winter ascent of Mount Marcy took place in what year?

A. 1893 (on snowshoes).

Q. What river is recognized as the best trout stream in New York?

A. Ausable.

———— ⋘ ————

Q. What upstate cities have American Hockey League franchises?

A. Albany, Glens Falls, Rochester, and Syracuse.

———— ⋘ ————

Q. Which Winter Olympic Games were the first held on man-made snow?

A. The 1932 Olympics in Lake Placid.

———— ⋘ ————

Q. What PGA Tour event celebrated its twenty-fifth anniversary in 1995?

A. The B.C. Open, at En-Joie Golf Club in Broome County.

———— ⋘ ————

Q. What famous wooden roller coaster, traditionally ranked among the top ten in the world, is located at the Great Escape?

A. The Comet.

———— ⋘ ————

Q. When was the first ski-jump competition held in Lake Placid?

A. In February 1921 (on the twenty-five-meter jump at Intervale).

———— ⋘ ————

Q. What is the nickname of the Rochester Americans professional hockey team?

A. The Amerks.

Q. The huge Windmill Farm and Craft Market near Penn Yan and its 250 vendors host how many annual visitors?

A. Four hundred thousand.

Q. What farm near the town of Gilboa offers week-long "work on the farm" vacations?

A. Golden Acres Farm and Ranch Resort.

Q. Abner Doubleday, legendary founder of baseball, was born in what town?

A. Auburn.

Q. What area of Lake Ontario is known as the Brown Trout Capital of the World?

A. Little Sodus Bay.

Q. Where were the 1980 PGA Championship, 1989 U.S. Open, and 1995 Ryder Cup golf matches played?

A. Oak Hill Country Club in Pittsford, outside Rochester.

Q. Visiting international businesspeople are known to flock to what popular attractions in western New York?

A. Wegmans grocery superstores.

Q. What famous Iron Man of baseball played minor-league ball with the Triple-A Rochester Red Wings?

A. Cal Ripken Jr.

Q. In what year did Army win its last college football national championship?

A. 1945.

———— ∞∞∞ ————

Q. How many travel-related businesses are operating in New York?

A. Fifty-three thousand.

———— ∞∞∞ ————

Q. What golfer and doctor won the 1956 U.S. Open Championship at Oak Hill Country Club, near Rochester?

A. Dr. Cary Middlecoff.

———— ∞∞∞ ————

Q. What is the seating capacity of Yankee Stadium, home of the New York Yankees?

A. 57,545.

———— ∞∞∞ ————

Q. Where is the National Soccer Hall of Fame located?

A. Oneonta.

———— ∞∞∞ ————

Q. Where is the U.S. Open Tennis Tournament played?

A. Flushing Meadow, in New York City.

———— ∞∞∞ ————

Q. The finals for college basketball's National Invitational Tournament are played in what arena?

A. New York City's Madison Square Garden.

Q. Former Buffalo area resident Jay Sigel won the U.S. Amateur Golf Championship in what two consecutive years?

A. 1982 and 1983.

Q. The Binghamton Rangers of the American Hockey League moved to what city after the 1997 season?

A. Hartford.

Q. What is the name of the ball-catching fan, who, at the age of twelve, briefly became a national celebrity after helping the New York Yankees win Game One of the 1996 American League championship series against Baltimore?

A. Jeff Maier.

Q. What race track opened in 1897?

A. Steeplechase Park, at Coney Island.

Q. What was the final score of the 1995 Ryder Cup Golf Matches at Oak Hill Country Club between the U.S. team and the European team?

A. Europe 14½, U.S. 13½.

Q. In what year did Jackie Robinson sign with the Brooklyn Dodgers, becoming the first African-American major-league baseball player?

A. 1947.

Q. What longtime "voice of the New York Yankees" died at age eighty-three on June 16, 1996?

A. Mel Allen.

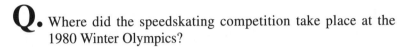

Q. Where did the speedskating competition take place at the 1980 Winter Olympics?

A. The oval at Lake Placid High School.

Q. What famous sportscaster was born in New York City on March 22, 1952, and later attended Syracuse University?

A. Bob Costas.

Q. What native of Lake Placid won the 1941 U.S. Open Golf Championship and has a course named after him in his hometown?

A. Craig Wood.

Q. What racquet sport was invented in Westchester County?

A. Platform tennis.

Q. What is the Double-A farm team for the New York Mets?

A. The Binghamton Mets.

Q. What is recognized as the second-oldest golf club in the United States?

A. Saint Andrews, in Westchester County.

Q. Where did Boog Powell, one of the most popular Baltimore Orioles of all time, play in the minor leagues?

A. With the Rochester Red Wings of the International League.

───── ∞∞∞ ─────

Q. Who was the longtime commissioner of the National Football League who made his home in Westchester?

A. Pete Rozelle.

───── ∞∞∞ ─────

Q. Where will you find the only antique carousel in the United States still housed at its original location?

A. The 1905 Dentzel menagerie carousel at Ontario Beach Park, in Monroe County.

───── ∞∞∞ ─────

Q. What team won the 1996 World Series?

A. The New York Yankees.

───── ∞∞∞ ─────

Q. What famous Russian pairs skater died tragically at age twenty-eight in 1995 while practicing in Lake Placid?

A. Sergei Grinkov.

───── ∞∞∞ ─────

Q. As of 1997, how many times had the Buffalo Bills gone to, and lost, the Super Bowl?

A. Four.

───── ∞∞∞ ─────

Q. Where is the Baseball Hall of Fame located?

A. Cooperstown.

Q. What is the name of the new Syracuse ballpark, opened in 1997 and home to the Syracuse Sky Chiefs of the Triple-A International League?

A. P&C Stadium.

Q. In what year did the American Football League grant a franchise to the Buffalo Bills?

A. 1959.

Q. Since 1975, how many times has Ithaca College won the Division III National Championship in football?

A. Three (1979, 1988, and 1991).

Q. What golf facility is the site of the Buick Classic on the PGA Tour?

A. Westchester Country Club.

Q. In what year were Buffalo's famous chicken wings first served at the Anchor Bar?

A. 1964.

Q. As of 1997, how many times had the Buffalo Sabres of the National Hockey League won the Stanley Cup Championship?

A. None (they lost in the 1974–75 finals to Philadelphia).

Q. How many outlet stores will you find at the Niagara International Factory Outlet Mall?

A. More than 150.

Q. What Triple-A baseball team was scheduled to move from the American Association to the International League in 1998?

A. The Buffalo Bisons.

Q. What is the name of the Rochester franchise in the National Lacrosse League?

A. Rochester Knighthawks.

Q. What is the home of the "Beef on Wick" sandwich (roast beef on crusty salted roll)?

A. Buffalo.

Q. What Westchester area country club hosts an annual Senior PGA Tour event?

A. Sleepy Hollow Country Club.

Q. What cruise boat has given tours of Buffalo Harbor and the Niagara River for more than twenty-five years?

A. The *Miss Buffalo*.

Q. What is New York State's largest campground?

A. Darien Lake, with more than two thousand campsites.

Q. How many visitors come to New York City each year?

A. More than twenty-five million.

Q. From what country do the greatest number of tourists come to visit New York State each year?

A. Canada.

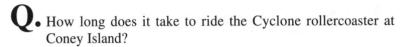

Q. How long does it take to ride the Cyclone rollercoaster at Coney Island?

A. One minute, fifty seconds.

Q. What cruise company has been taking visitors to the base of Niagara Falls for more than one hundred years?

A. *Maid of the Mist.*

Q. What is the nation's oldest horse-racing track?

A. Saratoga Race Course (built in 1865).

Q. What is the seating capacity of Rich Stadium, home of the Buffalo Bills?

A. 80,290.

Q. How many runners participate in the New York City Marathon each year?

A. Twenty-eight thousand.

Q. Where is the world's only golf driving range built on a pier?

A. The Chelsea Piers Sports & Entertainment Complex, in New York City.

Q. The infield of the Saratoga Race Course is the burial place for what famous race horse?

A. Go for Wand.

Q. What is the home course for the LPGA's Rochester International Tournament?

A. Locust Hill Country Club.

Q. What is the seating capacity of Shea Stadium, home of the New York Mets?

A. 55,601.

Q. What upstate New York team played in the North American Soccer League in the 1970s?

A. The Rochester Lancers.

Q. What former franchise of the Continental Basketball Association played in Albany?

A. The Albany Patroons.

Q. What was the original name of the Great Escape theme park in Lake George?

A. Storytown.

Q. Who are the Pelham residents who owned famed race horses Riva Ridge and Secretariat?

A. Christopher and Penny Chenery.

Q. How many people visit New York State annually?

A. Eighty million.

———∞———

Q. According to legend, in what year was the first-ever baseball game played in Cooperstown?

A. 1839.

———∞———

Q. How long is the Old Forge–to–Saranac Lake canoe route?

A. Approximately one hundred miles.

———∞———

Q. Where is the nation's oldest state park?

A. The Niagara Reservation.

———∞———

Q. What is the largest bathing-facility complex in the world?

A. Jones Beach, on Long Island.

———∞———

Q. What upstate college basketball team won the Division III National Championship in 1990?

A. University of Rochester.

———∞———

Q. New York State is home to how many state-operated swimming pools?

A. Twenty-four.

Q. What two cities provided the start and finish for the first long-distance automobile race in the United States?

A. New York City and Buffalo (September 1901).

———— ∞ ————

Q. What was the first sports facility in the nation to charge admission for a baseball game?

A. New York Fashion Race Track, on Long Island (July 20, 1858).

———— ∞ ————

Q. What was the first baseball team in America to travel and play in different cities?

A. The Brooklyn Excelsiors, in 1860.

———— ∞ ————

Q. Who won NBA Rookie of the Year honors in 1955–56 but had his career tragically cut short due to a debilitating illness?

A. Maurice Stokes, of the Rochester Royals.

———— ∞ ————

Q. Built in 1929 and used through the 1996 baseball season, Rochester's Silver Stadium was the "architectural twin" of what other stadium?

A. Cooper Stadium, in Columbus, Ohio.

———— ∞ ————

Q. What was the first indoor ski slope to open in the United States?
A. The Ski-Dek Center in Buffalo (in 1962).

———— ∞ ————

Q. After forming in 1897, where was the first tournament of the Intercollegiate Golf Association played?

A. Ardsley Casino Golf Club at Ardsley-on-Hudson.

Q. Where did a snowmobile first exceed a speed of 125 miles per hour?

A. At the Boonville Airport (on February 11, 1972).

———∞∞∞———

Q. How many state beaches are there in New York?

A. Seventy-six.

———∞∞∞———

Q. What is the seating capacity of Buffalo's North AmeriCare baseball park?

A. 21,050.

———∞∞∞———

Q. How many people visit the Empire State Building each year?

A. 2.5 million.

———∞∞∞———

Q. Who was the first bowler in America to roll two perfect three hundred games in a row in a sanctioned league competition?

A. Frank Caruana, of Buffalo (March 5, 1924).

———∞∞∞———

Q. What Westchester County park was one of the world's largest amusement parks in the late-1800s?

A. Glen Island.

———∞∞∞———

Q. Where did the first U.S. heavyweight fight to last more than one hundred rounds take place?

A. Caldwell's Landing (September 9, 1841; Hyer defeated McChester in 101 rounds).

Q. When was the National Baseball Hall of Fame in Cooperstown dedicated?

A. June 12, 1939.

Q. What was the first horse ever to win the Triple Crown?

A. Sir Barton (finishing up at Belmont Park in 1919).

Q. Who was the first bicycle racer to attain a speed of a mile per minute?

A. Charles Murphy (on June 30, 1899, in Farmingdale).

Q. The first National Wheelchair Games were held at what site?

A. Adelphi College, in Garden City (1957).

Q. In 1972, what legendary amateur player was clocked pitching a softball eighty-seven miles per hour in sanctioned league play?

A. Tommy "Rocket" Rosser of Amsterdam.

Q. Beginning in 1665, the first regular horse races in America ran at what track?

A. Newmarket Course, at Hempstead Plains on Long Island.

Q. Where was the American Canoe Association formed?

A. At Lake George (on August 3, 1880).

Q. Where were the first two- and four-man bobsled competitions in America held?

A. In Lake Placid (during the 1932 Winter Olympics).

Q. Where was the first Professional Golfers Association tournament in America held?

A. At Siwanoy Golf Club, in Mount Vernon (October 1916).

Q. TopFlite golf balls are manufactured by Spalding in what upstate community?

A. Johnstown.

Q. Going over Niagara Falls in a barrel was first dared by whom?

A. Anna Edson Taylor (October 24, 1901).

Q. What Rochester-born professional golfer won the 1988 PGA Championship?

A. Jeff Sluman.

Q. New York Yankees legends Babe Ruth and Billy Martin are both buried in what Westchester County cemetery?

A. Gate of Heaven Cemetery.

Q. What golf club has been awarded the 2003 PGA Championship?

A. Oak Hill Country Club, in Rochester.

Q. What type of racing served as a demonstration sport during the 1932 Winter Olympics in Lake Placid?

A. Dogsled.

———⊗⊗⊗———

Q. Who was the first player to score more than fifteen thousand points in his National Basketball Association career?

A. Dolph Schayes (of the Syracuse Nationals).

———⊗⊗⊗———

Q. What state park is the only one that offers an outdoor performing arts center, mineral bathhouses, and a championship golf course?

A. Saratoga Spa State Park.

———⊗⊗⊗———

Q. What former guard with the Rochester Royals of the NBA in the 1950s went on to coach the New York Knicks in the 1960s?

A. Red Holzman.

———⊗⊗⊗———

Q. What two LPGA Hall of Famers are multiple winners of the Rochester International golf tournament?

A. Nancy Lopez and Patty Sheehan.

———⊗⊗⊗———

Q. What upstate team was one of the six original members of the National Football League?

A. Rochester Jeffersons.

———⊗⊗⊗———

Q. How many state-operated golf courses are there in New York?

A. Twenty-three.

Q. As of 1997, how many times had the New York Rangers won the Stanley Cup?

A. Four (1928, 1933, 1940, and 1994).

Q. Who invented the steel-shafted golf club?

A. Arthur Knight (of Schenectady, in 1910).

Q. How many consecutive Stanley Cup championships did the New York Islanders win during the 1980s?

A. Four (1980–83).

Q. Who won college football's coach-of-the-year award for 1987?

A. Dick MacPherson, of Syracuse University.

Q. How much did it cost to stage the 1932 Winter Olympics in Lake Placid?

A. Less than one million dollars.

Q. Going into 1997, what pro golfer and resident of New Hartford had won twelve times on the PGA Tour?

A. Wayne Levi.

Q. How many state parks are there in New York?

A. 150.

Q. How many spectators attended the 1980 Winter Olympic games in Lake Placid?

A. Five hundred thousand.

Q. How many miles of hiking trails are there in the Adirondacks?

A. More than two thousand.

Q. How long is the Northville to Lake Placid hiking trail?

A. 130 miles.

Q. What facility used by a minor-league affiliate of the New York Mets is regarded as one of the best Double-A ballparks in the nation?

A. Binghamton Municipal Stadium.

Q. How many state campsites are there in New York?

A. 8,353.

Q. How many interconnected lakes and ponds are there in the Saint Regis canoe area?

A. Fifty-seven.

Q. According to the *Places Rated Almanac*, what is the sixth-best metro area in America for access to public golf courses?

A. Glens Falls.

Q. How many competitors participated in the 1932 Winter Olympics in Lake Placid?

A. Three hundred (from seventeen nations).

———⊗≋⊙———

Q. What did the New York Yankees originally start out as in 1901 before becoming the New York Highlanders in 1903 and the Yankees in 1912?

A. The Baltimore Orioles (moved to New York in 1903).

———⊗≋⊙———

Q. What is the largest publicly operated golf facility in the nation?

A. Bethpage State Park, on Long Island (five courses).

———⊗≋⊙———

Q. In what year did the New York Mets join baseball's National League?

A. 1962.

———⊗≋⊙———

Q. How many athletes competed in the 1980 Winter Olympic games in Lake Placid?

A. Sixteen hundred (from thirty-two countries).

———⊗≋⊙———

Q. According to the *Places Rated Almanac*, what is the fifth-best metro area in America for recreation?

A. Long Island.

———⊗≋⊙———

Q. How many public golf courses are there in the Albany-Schenectady-Troy metropolitan area?

A. Thirty.

Q. What collegiate Division One hockey team plays in Troy?

A. The Rensselaer Polytechnic (RPI) Engineers.

———⊸⊶⊸———

Q. Pro golfer Joey Sindelar grew up in what community?

A. Horseheads.

———⊸⊶⊸———

Q. For what minor-league affiliate of the New York Yankees did Whitey Ford and Thurman Munson both play?

A. The Binghamton Triplets.

———⊸⊶⊸———

Q. How many women athletes competed in the 1932 Winter Olympics at Lake Placid?

A. Thirty-two.

———⊸⊶⊸———

Q. What collegiate Division One basketball team plays at the Marine Midland Arena in Buffalo?

A. The Canisus College Golden Griffins.

———⊸⊶⊸———

Q. What did the Sacramento Kings of the National Basketball Association begin as before becoming the Cincinnati Royals and then the Kansas City Kings?

A. The Rochester Royals.

———⊸⊶⊸———

Q. How many female athletes competed in the 1980 Winter Olympics in Lake Placid?

A. Three hundred.

Q. From the back tees, how long is "the Monster" golf course at the Concord Resort, ranked by *Golf Digest* as one of America's best seventy-five resort courses?

A. 7, 471 yards.

Q. What small college in western New York fields a Division One basketball team and produced NBA Hall of Famer Calvin Murphy?

A. Niagara University (the Purple Eagles).

Q. What is the nickname of the Marist College Division One basketball team?

A. The Red Foxes.

Q. How many medals did the U.S. team win at the 1980 Winter Olympics in Lake Placid?

A. Twelve.

Q. According to the *Places Rated Almanac*, how many metro areas in New York are ranked in the top ten for access to public golf courses?

A. Four (Glens Falls, Jamestown, Binghamton, and Utica-Rome).

Q. What Division One college basketball team plays on Long Island?

A. The Hofstra University Flying Dutchmen.

Q. What was the A-League average attendance mark set by the professional soccer Rochester Rhinos during their inaugural season in 1996?

A. An average of more than eleven thousand fans per game.

Q. How many roller coasters will you find at Darien Lake?

A. Four (the Mind Eraser, the Predator, the Viper, and the Nightmare).

Q. What minor-league baseball and soccer stadium, opened in 1996, features train tracks just beyond the outfield, with passing trains providing extra entertainment for fans?

A. Frontier Field, in Rochester.

Q. What college basketball team has led the nation in attendance several times in the 1990s?

A. Syracuse University Orangemen (who play in the Carrier Dome).

Q. What is the nickname of the Division One college football team at Colgate University?

A. The Red Raiders.

Q. In what league does the Utica Blizzard professional hockey team play?

A. The Colonial League.

Q. What was the purse for the 1997 Corning Classic LPGA Tournament?

A. $650,000.

Q. What were the San Francisco Giants of the National League named in 1879, before moving to New York City in 1883?

A. The Troy Trojans.

Q. Lawrence Peter Berra of New York Yankees fame is better known by what name?

A. Yogi Berra.

Q. How much money is spent annually by visitors to New York State, according to the N.Y.S. Division of Tourism?

A. $13.1 billion.

Q. How many people are employed by the travel industry in New York?

A. More than six hundred thousand.

Q. The 1932 Winter Olympics in Lake Placid were watched by how many spectators?

A. Fifty thousand.

Q. What collegiate Division One basketball team plays in Albany?

A. The Siena College Saints.

Q. How many campgrounds are there in New York State?

A. Approximately five hundred.

Q. How many golf holes can you play at the Lake Placid Resort?

A. Forty-five (two eighteen-hole courses plus a nine-hole course).

Q. What Finger Lakes region college football team won the national championship in both 1921 and 1922?

A. Cornell.

Q. Who designed renowned golf courses in New York, such as the Sagamore in Bolton Landing and Oak Hill in Rochester?

A. Donald Ross.

Q. How much did it cost to stage the 1980 Winter Olympics in Lake Placid?

A. $175 million.

Q. Who was coach of the Rochester Royals when they won the NBA Championship in 1951?

A. Les Harrison.

Q. In what year did the Syracuse Nationals win the NBA Championship?

A. 1955.

Q. From what high school did 1988 PGA Champion Jeff Sluman graduate?

A. Greece Arcadia High School (1975).

Q. How many times has Syracuse University won the national championship of college football?

A. Once (1959).

Q. What historic thoroughbred racetrack is nicknamed the Graveyard of Champions due to its tendency for major upset victories by long shots?

A. Saratoga Race Course.

Q. New York State's only Formula One Grand Prix auto-racing venue is located where?

A. Watkins Glen.

Q. What was the first bikeway in the Adirondacks?

A. The Blue Mountain-to-Indian Lake bikeway (1977).

Q. What is the primary mode of transportation to some of the best fishing spots in the Adirondacks?

A. Seaplane (due to the isolation of some lakes).

Q. Who was the last New York college football player to win the Heisman Trophy?

A. Ernie Davis (of Syracuse, in 1961).

Q. What town is referred to as the Snowmobile Capital of the East?

A. Old Forge.

─────

Q. After winning the U.S. Open two months earlier, what golfer won the 1980 PGA Championship at Oak Hill Country Club at the age of forty?

A. Jack Nicklaus.

─────

Q. What is the nickname of the Class A Jamestown baseball team of the New York-Penn League?

A. The Jammers.

─────

Q. What New York college football player and current TV actor still holds the NCAA all-time record for the highest average yards rushed per game in a career?

A. Ed Marinaro (of Cornell; 174.6 yards per game, 1969–71).

─────

Q. How many miles of snowmobile trails are there in Hamilton County?

A. More than 750.

SCIENCE & NATURE

C H A P T E R   S I X

Q. What is New York's state bird?

A. The bluebird.

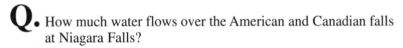

Q. How much water flows over the American and Canadian falls at Niagara Falls?

A. Approximately one hundred thousand cubic feet per second.

Q. Where is Corning Glass headquartered?

A. Corning.

Q. What area of New York State receives an average of more than two hundred inches of snow each winter?

A. The Tug Hill Plateau, east of Lake Ontario.

Q. What area of the Adirondacks is known as a home to the Timber Rattler?

A. Tongue Mountain, on Lake George.

Q. Where is the largest open-pit titanium mine in the world?

A. Tahawus.

———————

Q. When was the last cougar reportedly killed in New York?

A. In 1894 (in Hamilton County).

———————

Q. The Roberson Museum and Science Center & Link Planetarium is located in what city?

A. Binghamton.

———————

Q. At what age was the oldest wild bear ever caught in New York?

A. Forty-two (caught in 1974 near Newcomb).

———————

Q. Where was the first outdoor sanitarium to treat tuberculosis in the United States?

A. Saranac Lake (1884).

———————

Q. What was the first forest ranger school in the United States?

A. New York State Ranger School, near Cranberry Lake (in 1912).

———————

Q. Where was the first fire tower in the Adirondacks?

A. Mount Morris, in Franklin County (1909).

Q. What brewery is located in Rochester?

A. Genesee Brewing Company.

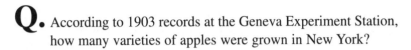

Q. According to 1903 records at the Geneva Experiment Station, how many varieties of apples were grown in New York?

A. 698.

Q. What is the snowiest *city* in the United States?

A. Syracuse (with an average yearly snowfall of 114 inches).

Q. What is New York State's only IMAX theater, featuring a sixty-six-foot-high, hemisphere-shaped screen?

A. The Bristol Omnitheater in Syracuse.

Q. What is New York's state flower?

A. The rose.

Q. On average, how many days per year does the temperature reach ninety degrees in Rochester?

A. Nine.

Q. Where is the National Technical Institute for the Deaf located?

A. On the campus of the Rochester Institute of Technology in Rochester.

Q. What caused some Long Island beaches to close for the summer in 1988?

A. Medical waste being dumped offshore.

———————

Q. How much did the biggest bear ever shot in New York weigh?

A. 750 pounds (shot in 1975 near Altamont in Franklin County).

———————

Q. What meteorological event took place in New York City on the day after Christmas 1947?

A. New York City was paralyzed by a 25.8-inch snowstorm.

———————

Q. What is one of the largest public access observatories in the Northeast?

A. The Kopernik Space Education Center, in Vestal.

———————

Q. What aviator became famous (infamous, actually) when, in 1938, he made a solo flight from New York City to Ireland, instead of to California as he had intended?

A. Douglas "Wrong-Way" Corrigan.

———————

Q. What is the average annual snowfall in Albany, New York State's capital?

A. 65.2 inches.

———————

Q. What is the highest temperature ever recorded in New York State?

A. 108 degrees, in Troy (on July 22, 1926).

Q. What is the lowest temperature ever recorded in New York State?

A. Minus fifty-two degrees in Old Forge (February 18, 1979).

———— ∞∞ ————

Q. Where was the Moog synthesizer, one of the first electronic musical instruments, invented?

A. Trumansburg.

———— ∞∞ ————

Q. What famous condiment maker is based in Rochester?

A. R. T. French.

———— ∞∞ ————

Q. What is the fifth-oldest zoo in the United States?

A. The Ross Park Zoo, in Binghamton.

———— ∞∞ ————

Q. What is the average rise and fall of tides in New York City?

A. Five feet, one inch.

———— ∞∞ ————

Q. According to state conservation authorities, as of 1989, what percentage of Adirondack lakes were so polluted with acid rain that fish could not survive?

A. 25 percent.

———— ∞∞ ————

Q. Who is the McIntosh apple (more commonly known as "Macs") named for?

A. John MacIntosh, a native of Albany (yes, the names are spelled differently).

Q. What are the average wind speed and highest wind speed recorded in Buffalo?

A. 11.9 miles per hour average; 91 miles per hour.

———⊗⊗⊗———

Q. According to the Environmental Protection Agency, how many hazardous waste sites were identified in New York State in 1996?

A. Seventy-nine.

———⊗⊗⊗———

Q. How many species of animals inhabit the Buffalo Zoo?

A. 180.

———⊗⊗⊗———

Q. Where was the first lumbering operation in the Adirondacks?

A. At the mouth of the Saranac River.

———⊗⊗⊗———

Q. What company was the first to manufacture perforated toilet paper?

A. The Albany Perforated Wrapping Paper Company (in 1874).

———⊗⊗⊗———

Q. Bausch & Lomb has its world headquarters in what city?

A. Rochester.

———⊗⊗⊗———

Q. When was the last major tornado to hit New York State?

A. November 16, 1989 (in Newburgh; nine deaths).

Q. Where was the first rocket plane designed to carry a human built in the United States?

A. In Buffalo (by the Bell Aircraft Corporation in 1946).

———∞∞∞———

Q. Who invented the first flight simulator?

A. Edwin A. Link (of Broome County).

———∞∞∞———

Q. How many people were killed in the March 25, 1990, fire at a Bronx social club?

A. Eighty-seven.

———∞∞∞———

Q. How long did Robert Fulton's first steamboat trip take in 1807, covering the 150 miles from New York City to Albany?

A. Thirty-two hours.

———∞∞∞———

Q. What is the average annual attendance at the Bronx Zoo?

A. Two million.

———∞∞∞———

Q. The Cutler Botanical Gardens is located where?

A. Binghamton.

———∞∞∞———

Q. Where is the largest McIntosh apple orchard in the world?

A. Clinton County.

Q. What was the first steamboat to sail on the Great Lakes?

A. *Walk-in-the-Water* (sailed from Buffalo to Detroit in 1818).

Q. Approximately one-half of the people employed nationally in the manufacturing of photographic equipment and supplies work in what upstate New York city?

A. Rochester.

Q. In what Westchester County community was the cocktail invented?

A. Elmsford.

Q. Where was the nation's first commercial winery?

A. Croton-on-Hudson.

Q. The world's only Ph.D. program for imaging science is located at what New York university?

A. The Rochester Institute of Technology.

Q. What was the hometown of Frank and Homer Anderson, inventors of the first typewriter to use both uppercase and lowercase letters?

A. Peekskill.

Q. What West Landing resident completed the nation's first telegraph lines and founded Cornell University?

A. Ezra Cornell.

Q. In 1885, one of the first streetcars in the nation began operating in what upstate city?

A. Ithaca.

Q. What woman aviator was a former resident of Harrison?

A. Amelia Earhart.

Q. Who was the one-time Peekskill resident who invented the method for quick-freezing ice cream?

A. Edwin Lockwood.

Q. What hospital was the first in the nation to have a diagnostic and treatment center for Lyme disease?

A. The Westchester County Medical Center.

Q. How many alumni of the Rochester Institute of Technology have won Pulitzer Prizes in photography?

A. Eight.

Q. What Westchester resident was the inventor of the transatlantic cable?

A. Cyrus Field.

Q. Who was the late Port Chester resident who led the stone-carving effort on Mount Rushmore?

A. Luigi DelBianco.

Q. Credited for taking the first photographs of the moon, what late Hastings-on-Hudson resident founded New York University's School of Medicine?

A. Dr. John William Draper.

Q. Yorktown was home to what frozen-food millionaire?

A. Clarence Birdseye.

Q. Sleepy Hollow Cemetery is the final resting place for what automobile industry giant?

A. Walter Chrysler.

Q. Where is one of the nation's first commercially operated nuclear power plants located?

A. Indian Point.

Q. Where is the Andrus Space Planetarium located?

A. Yonkers.

Q. What huge computer manufacturer traces its roots to Broome County?

A. IBM.

Q. What lake is home to the reputed sea monster Champ?

A. Champlain.

Q. The nation's largest laser in an educational setting can be found at what New York university?

A. The University of Rochester.

———∞———

Q. What is the birthplace of Jell-O?

A. LeRoy (where Pearl Wait created it in 1897).

———∞———

Q. What popular condiment was first produced by the R. T. French Company of Rochester in 1904?

A. Prepared mustard.

———∞———

Q. In what city did a thirty-pound meteorite hit a parked car in October 1992?

A. Peekskill.

———∞———

Q. What company that now "brings good things to life" was founded in Schenectady in 1889?

A. The Edison General Electric Company (now GE).

———∞———

Q. What is the largest state-operated museum in the nation?

A. The New York State Museum, at the Empire State Plaza in Albany.

———∞———

Q. Where was the material used to replace ivory in the production of billiard balls developed?

A. In Albany, by the Hyatt M. Manufacturing Company (in 1868).

Q. What four world-class optics-oriented corporations started out in Rochester?

A. Eastman Kodak, Xerox, Bausch & Lomb, and Gannett Newspapers.

Q. Where in America was pie à la mode first served?

A. At the Cambridge Hotel in Washington County.

Q. In what year did A. Pagenstecher discover the process for grinding wood into pulp to make paper, leading to the eventual establishment of International Paper at Lake Luzerne?

A. 1869.

Q. Where did the first television broadcast in America to a private home take place?

A. In Schenectady (in 1928).

Q. Two mummies have been on display at what location since 1831?

A. At the Albany Institute of History and Art.

Q. Who created the world's first fountain pen?

A. Absalom Bishop and Thayer Codding (of Rochester, in 1849).

Q. In what upstate zoo will you find a rare red panda?

A. The Buffalo Zoo.

Q. Where will you find the world's largest Japanese cherry tree?

A. At the New York Botanical Garden in New York City.

Q. Which of the world's Eight Modern Wonders is located in New York City?

A. The Empire State Building.

Q. What was the major industry on Long Island in the early 1700s?

A. Whaling.

Q. In what year did fires destroy large portions of the Catskill and Adirondack forests?

A. 1924.

Q. Who developed celluloid, which was widely used in the production of game pieces for checkers, dominos, and children's building blocks?

A. John Wesley Hyatt (of Albany, in the mid-1800s).

Q. What is the state tree?

A. The sugar maple.

Q. Where was America's first gold tooth developed and used?

A. In Rochester (Dr. J. B. Beers, in 1843).

Q. What is the name of the National Wildlife Refuge near Auburn?

A. Montezuma.

Q. From what stone was the State Capitol building made?

A. Granite.

Q. Where was the first state nature center in the United States?

A. The Trailside Museum, at Bear Mountain.

Q. In what upstate New York city was Western Union founded in 1857?

A. Rochester (by Hiram Sibley).

Q. What was the first laboratory in America established exclusively for the study of cancer?

A. The New York State Pathological Laboratory (in 1898).

Q. How many nature centers does New York State operate?

A. Sixteen.

Q. Joseph Henry, "Father of the Telegraph," lived and worked in what city?

A. Albany.

Q. How many species of fish can be found in the Adirondack Park?

A. Eighty-six.

———⊗⊗⊙———

Q. In what city was the Fuller Brush Company of door-to-door notoriety founded?

A. Schenectady.

———⊗⊗⊙———

Q. What was the peak year for Hudson River logging?

A. 1872 (213.8 million feet of lumber was milled).

———⊗⊗⊙———

Q. What is the Iroquois word for "bark eater"?

A. *Rat-i-ron-tack* (the inspiration for "Adirondacks").

———⊗⊗⊙———

Q. What Buffalo-based company began selling homemade pasta in 1910?

A. Gioia Macaroni.

———⊗⊗⊙———

Q. The nation's largest unclassified major fusion laboratory is located where?

A. The Laboratory for Laser Energetics at the University of Rochester.

———⊗⊗⊙———

Q. Who invented the rolltop desk?

A. Abner Cutler (of Buffalo, in 1850).

Q. What connected Glens Falls with Fort Edward, allowing the transport of logs around waterfalls on the Hudson River?

A. The eight-mile-long Glens Falls Feeder Canal.

Q. For what is Green Lake State Park famous?

A. The turquoise waters of Green Lake.

Q. Where was the first dental chair invented?

A. In Rochester (by Frank Ritter, in 1887).

Q. In what year did a massive snowstorm take place that Buffalo residents refer to simply as "the Blizzard"?

A. 1977.

Q. Where was the first modern globe-making facility in America?

A. At 110 Washington Street in Albany (beginning in 1815).

Q. What is the official state muffin?

A. The apple muffin.

Q. What was the real name of Johnny Appleseed, who planted his first orchard in Olean?

A. John Chapman.

Q. Rochester native Jesse Hatch developed what type of footwear in the 1840s?

A. Baby shoes.

Q. Where was cellophane invented?

A. In Buffalo (by Du Pont, in 1924).

Q. What claimant to the discovery of the North Pole is buried in Buffalo's Forest Lawn cemetery?

A. Frederick Cook.

Q. What locomotive was the first in the nation to attain the verified speed of 112.5 miles per hour?

A. The *Empire State Express* locomotive 999 (in 1893).

Q. During its operation from 1830 to 1859, what lighthouse in America was the first to be fueled by natural gas?

A. Barcelona Harbor, on Lake Erie.

Q. What was the first farm bureau in the United States?

A. The Broome County Farm Bureau (established in 1913).

Q. Who invented oleomargarine?

A. Henry Bradley (of Binghamton, in 1871).

Q. How many species of trees will you find in the Adirondacks?

A. Thirty.

———— ∞∞ ————

Q. What is the state fish?

A. The brook, or speckled, trout.

———— ∞∞ ————

Q. Who manufactured the first practical motorcycle?

A. The E. R. Thomas Motor Company (of Buffalo, in 1900).

———— ∞∞ ————

Q. Who was the first U.S. woman architect?

A. Louise Bethune (of Buffalo; she opened an office in 1881).

———— ∞∞ ————

Q. Where and when was the first college radio station broadcast?

A. Union College (in Schenectady, in 1921).

———— ∞∞ ————

Q. What upstate New York–based company manufactured the world's first synthetic vitamin A?

A. Eastman Kodak.

———— ∞∞ ————

Q. Where was the first power knitting machine in America put into operation?

A. In Cohoes (by Egberts and Bailey, 1832).

Q. In 1992, what upstate New York community was chosen by the National Science Foundation to be the home of the Center for Electronic Imaging?

A. Rochester.

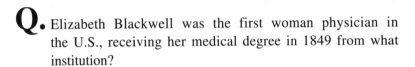

Q. Elizabeth Blackwell was the first woman physician in the U.S., receiving her medical degree in 1849 from what institution?

A. The Medical Institution of Geneva (later Syracuse University Medical School).

Q. Since Niagara Falls was first visited by Europeans in 1678, how far has it moved upstream?

A. About one thousand feet.

Q. What community became infamous for settling on top of a toxic waste dump?

A. Love Canal, in Niagara Falls.

Q. What is the nation's largest manufacturer of tailored men's clothing?

A. Hickey-Freeman of Rochester.

Q. The flour used to make graham crackers was developed by whom?

A. Sylvester Graham (of Rochester, in the late-1800s).

Q. In terms of New York farm income, what are the three biggest agricultural products?

A. Cheese, butter, and milk.

Q. The first airplane to fly at least five hundred miles took off from Chicago on November 19, 1916, and landed where?

A. Hornell, New York (actually 590 miles).

Q. Where was the first solid-state electronic computer built?

A. In Ilion (by the Sperry Rand Corporation, in 1958).

Q. Who coined the word *typewriter*?

A. Inventor Christopher Sholes (of Ilion, in 1868).

Q. What type of bird was hatched and reared in captivity for the first time in America in Ithaca in 1934?

A. The ptarmigan (also referred to as the Eskimo chicken).

Q. What New Rochelle resident invented the streetcar?

A. John Stephenson.

Q. What college offers the only bachelor of science degree in microelectronics engineering in the United States?

A. The Rochester Institute of Technology.

Q. Who invented the paper clip?

A. Clarence Collette, of Schenectady.

———∞∞∞———

Q. Where were gloves first commercially manufactured in the United States?

A. In Johnstown (1809).

———∞∞∞———

Q. Where was the first rope-operated inclined railway in America constructed for use in transporting military supplies?

A. Lewiston (near Niagara Falls, in 1764 by British troops).

———∞∞∞———

Q. What upstate attraction is recognized as one of the finest planetariums in the nation?

A. The Strasenburgh Planetarium, at the Rochester Museum and Science Center.

———∞∞∞———

Q. Who invented shredded-wheat biscuits?

A. Henry Perky and William Ford (of Watertown, in 1893).

———∞∞∞———

Q. Freeze-dried coffee was first made available nationally in 1968 by what company?

A. General Foods, of White Plains.

———∞∞∞———

Q. What body of water is referred to as America's Sixth Great Lake?

A. Lake Champlain.

Q. For what is the Adirondack Visitor Interpretive Center in Newcomb known?

A. Spectacular views of the High Peaks.

———— ∞ ————

Q. How many farms are there in Hamilton County?

A. None (due to the very short growing season and topography).

———— ∞ ————

Q. Where was milk first pasteurized commercially in the United States?

A. In Bloomville (by the Sheffield Farms Company, in 1895).

———— ∞ ————

Q. What county in the Adirondack region has seen frost in every month of the year?

A. Hamilton County.

———— ∞ ————

Q. What is the Hudson Valley's only zoo?

A. The Catskill Game Farm.

———— ∞ ————

Q. The long, narrow Finger Lakes, created by the retreating glaciers in the Ice Age, resulted in an environment ideal for the production of what?

A. Wine.

———— ∞ ————

Q. How many Canadian geese migrate annually to the Montezuma Wildlife Refuge outside Auburn?

A. Approximately seventy thousand.

Q. On average, how many inches of snow does the town of Webb in Herkimer County, one of the snowiest towns east of the Rockies, get each winter season?

A. 270 inches (or about twenty-three feet).

———∞∞∞———

Q. How many lakes are there in the Fulton Chain Lakes?

A. Eight.

———∞∞∞———

Q. Where was the first all-electric house built?

A. In Schenectady (at the General Electric plot in 1903).

———∞∞∞———

Q. A wine tank at the Taylor Winery in Hammondsport, formerly used to hold thirty-five thousand gallons of fermenting wine, is now used for what?

A. As a movie theater that depicts the history of the wineries.

———∞∞∞———

Q. How many falls are there at Niagara?

A. Three (Canadian, American, and Bridal Veil).

———∞∞∞———

Q. When the Adirondacks were first populated in the 1800s, what was the area's biggest industry?

A. Lumber.

———∞∞∞———

Q. At what museum can you see exhibits on the 435-million-year geologic history of the Niagara gorge?

A. The Schoellkopf Geological Museum, at the Niagara Reservation State Park.

Q. Where was the voting machine invented?

A. In Rochester (in 1889).

Q. At what Niagara Falls location can you see hundreds of flowering plants in the middle of winter?

A. The Wintergarden (a glass-enclosed botanical garden).

Q. What is the fifth-largest power-generating project in the world?

A. The New York Power Authority Niagara Project.

Q. What western New York community boasts five levels of locks on the Barge Canal?

A. Lockport.

Q. At what museum can you find Seneca Indian artifacts dating back to 1550?

A. The Rochester Museum and Science Center.

Q. In what community can you find the Hoffman Clock Museum, one of only four clock museums in the United States?

A. Newark.

Q. When completed in 1825, what was considered the largest structure of its type in the world?

A. The Erie Canal aqueduct over the Genesee River (eight hundred feet long).

Q. What museum in western New York boasts the largest collection of dolls in the world?

A. The Strong Museum in Rochester (nearly twenty thousand).

Q. Where were the first thermometers in the United States manufactured?

A. In Rochester (by George Taylor and David Kendall, in 1851).

Q. What is considered to be the nation's third-largest living historic village?

A. Genesee Country Village and Museum, in Mumford.

Q. At what fifty-acre Victorian garden estate will you find nine formal gardens, including one of the largest displays of roses in the state?

A. Sonnenberg Gardens, in Canandaigua.

Q. What is considered to be the largest bicycle museum in the world?

A. Pedaling History, in Buffalo.

Q. How many gallons of water are displaced at the Eisenhower Lock in the Saint Lawrence Seaway when a cargo ship is lowered forty feet?

A. Twenty-two million gallons!

Q. Who was responsible for introducing grape growing to Hammondsport by transplanting grapevines from the Hudson Valley in 1829 to produce wine for parishioners?

A. Reverend William Bostwick.

Q. What famed aviator from the Finger Lakes region designed the first airplane ever purchased by the U.S. Navy and now has a museum in his honor outside of Hammondsport?

A. Glen Curtiss.

Q. What town is known as the world's largest producer of buckwheat products?

A. Penn Yan, in the Finger Lakes region.

Q. Seneca Lake, the deepest of the Finger Lakes, is how deep?

A. 650 feet.

Q. At Watkins Glen State Park, how many stone steps must one descend along the mile-and-a-half gorge trail to the bottom?

A. Eight hundred.

Q. What is the state gem?

A. Garnet.

Q. In what community can you see more than a dozen historic gliders and sailplanes on display?

A. In Elmira, at the National Soaring Museum.

Q. Where were marshmallows first mass-produced for commercial sale?

A. In Rochester (by Joseph Demerath, in 1895).

Q. At what museum can you find a large collection of World War II and Korean conflict warplanes, as well as the annual Wings of Eagles Air Show in August?

A. The National Warplane Museum, in Geneseo.

———∞∞———

Q. Buffalo industrialist William Pryor Letchworth fought to preserve what spectacular river gorge in the 1870s, resulting in a state park there being named for him?

A. The Genesee River gorge (Letchworth State Park).

———∞∞———

Q. What Washington County community is sometimes called the "slate capital of the world"?

A. Granville.

———∞∞———

Q. How long did it take fifty craftsmen working six-day weeks to complete construction of the Romanesque mansion Belhurst Castle on the shore of Seneca Lake?

A. Four years.

———∞∞———

Q. For what crop is Washington County famous?

A. Apples.

———∞∞———

Q. Where was the turret for the battleship *Monitor* built?

A. In Schenectady (by Clute Brothers).

———∞∞———

Q. Who invented the mail chute for use in office buildings?

A. James Cutler (of Rochester, in 1889).

Q. What is the state beverage?

A. Milk.

Q. The nuns of the New Skete Monastery in Cambridge have gained famed by producing what delicious dessert item?

A. Cheesecake.

Q. At what museum can you find specimens of long-vanished wildlife from the Adirondack region?

A. The Pember Museum of Natural History, in Granville.

Q. In what suburb of Rochester does Xerox manufacture its copiers?

A. Webster.

Q. On a clear day, how many mountain peaks can supposedly be seen from the thirty-eight-hundred-foot summit of Blue Mountain in the Adirondacks?

A. 165.

Q. In what year was the first spring log drive in the Adirondacks, along the Schroon River?

A. 1813 (by Alanson and Norman Fox of Brant Lake).

Q. How many black bears live in the Adirondack region?

A. Approximately four thousand.

Q. At what museum can you find exhibits about the first American warships used in the Revolutionary War?

A. The Skenesborough Museum, in Whitehall.

———— ∞∞ ————

Q. For what use did British troops during the 1700s cut down white pines that lined the shores of Lake George and Lake Champlain?

A. To serve as masts for British naval ships.

———— ∞∞ ————

Q. The Steuben Glass Factory, producer of some of the finest glass objects in the world, is located where?

A. It is part of the Corning Glass Center, in Corning.

———— ∞∞ ————

Q. What is the only major aquarium in upstate New York?

A. The Aquarium of Niagara, in Niagara Falls.

———— ∞∞ ————

Q. What famous humorist and writer has a state park named for him outside of Elmira?

A. Mark Twain.

———— ∞∞ ————

Q. How many state recreation areas are there on Long Island?

A. Twenty-four.

———— ∞∞ ————

Q. How much snow does the Buffalo metropolitan area get in an average winter?

A. 91.1 inches.

Q. The telescope mirror of the Palomar Observatory in California, the largest piece of glass in the world, was manufactured by what company?

A. Corning Glass, in 1937.

Q. How many species of mammals are there in the Adirondack Park?

A. Fifty-five.

Q. At one time in the mid-1800s, what was known as "the horseshoe capital of the world"?

A. The Burden Iron Works, in Troy.

Q. In what county was the nation's first factory-produced cheese made in 1851?

A. Oneida County.

Q. How many days in an average year does the temperature dip below freezing in Buffalo?

A. 131.

Q. How many inches of snow does Binghamton get in an average winter?

A. 82.4 inches.

Q. Where is the largest garnet mine in the world located?

A. Near North Creek, in the central Adirondacks.

Q. What natural attraction is located near Pottersville?

A. The Natural Stone Bridge and Caves.

Q. How many species of birds are there in the Adirondack Park?

A. 218.

Q. What natural attraction is located just west of Saratoga Springs?

A. The Petrified Sea Gardens.

Q. When Eastman Kodak founder George Eastman took his own life in 1932, what did his note to friends say?

A. "My work is done. Why wait?"

Q. Contrary to popular belief, what city has the sunniest summers in the entire state?

A. Buffalo.

Q. What did the Flint Glass Company become when it moved from Brooklyn to Corning in 1868?

A. Corning Glass.

Q. What conservation and recreation organization celebrated its seventy-fifth anniversary in 1997?

A. The Adirondack Mountain Club.

Q. What inventor was born in 1878, worked for a time at General Electric in Schenectady, and is credited as a television pioneer in the 1920s?

A. Ernst Alexanderson.

———⌘———

Q. What famed aviator was born in Warrensburg in 1890 and flew over the North Pole with Richard E. Byrd in 1926?

A. Floyd Bennett.

———⌘———

Q. What inventor developed the photoelectric process that would eventually lead to the founding of the Haloid (later Xerox) Corporation in Rochester?

A. Chester Floyd Carlson.

———⌘———

Q. How many species of reptiles and amphibians are there in the Adirondacks?

A. Thirty-five.

———⌘———

Q. In what year did Thomas Edison move his electrical machine works from New York City to Schenectady?

A. 1886.

———⌘———

Q. At what museum will you find a display of more than twenty-two thousand glass objects?

A. The Corning Glass Center, in Corning.

———⌘———

Q. The Empire apple, introduced in 1966, is a cross between what other two popular types of apples?

A. McIntosh and Red Delicious.

Q. What were "corduroy roads" used in some parts of the Adirondacks made from?

A. Logs semiburied across the width of the trail (the alternative was mud).

———❧———

Q. How many gallons of maple sap must be collected, condensed by boiling, and then evaporated in order to produce one gallon of New York's famous maple syrup?

A. Forty.

———❧———

Q. What is the duration of New York State's apple season?

A. August through October.

———❧———

Q. Where does New York State rank nationally in terms of grape and wine production?

A. Second (behind California).

———❧———

Q. What combination of natural elements accounts for New York State's spectacular fall foliage from mid-September to mid-October?

A. Warm days, cool nights, and the great variety of broad-leaved trees.

———❧———

Q. What county is the largest producer of milk in the state?

A. Cayuga.

———❧———

Q. How many vineyards are there in New York State?

A. Eleven hundred.

Q. What used to be at the base of the thousand-foot-high Helderberg Escarpment near Albany?

A. The floor of an ancient sea.

Q. How many pounds of apples are produced in state-leader Wayne County each year?

A. Approximately 370 million.

Q. In what town was the first commercially successful system of sound film invented in 1923?

A. Auburn (at the Case Research Lab).

Q. How many major waterfalls higher than fifty feet are located within Letchworth State Park?

A. Three.

Q. How many wineries are there in New York State?

A. Approximately one hundred.

Q. When do leaves begin to turn colors in the Adirondack region?

A. As early as late-August.

Q. What portion of New York State's grape production is used for wine production?

A. Only half (the other half is used to make grape juice).